Helping America Help Itself

Whipporwill Press,
    Helping America Help Itself: Westlake Hardware/[Jack Cashill], — 1st. ed.
    p. cm.
    ISBN : 0-9741968-1-9

1. Westlake Ace Hardware—History. 2. Hardware industry.
I. Westlake Ace Hardware.
II. Title.

Library of Congress Control Number: 2005927911

Printed and bound in the United States of America

Westlake Ace Hardware
14000 Marshall Drive
Lenexa, Kansas 66215
Phone: 913-888-8438
www.westlakehardware.com

CREDITS:

Westlake Ace Hardware

Kevin Pfeifer
Director of Advertising and Sales Promotion

Linda Smith
Manager of Corporate Communications

Consultants

Book Producer:	Ron Daniel Firefly Marketing Communications
Research and writing:	Jack Cashill
Dust jacket and book design:	Desiree Mueller Firefly Marketing Communications

Table of Contents

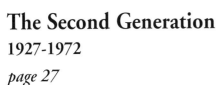

A lasting legacy for generations to come

W.I. Westlake's goal of taking a leadership role in hardware sales and merchandising was a dream realized far beyond the boundaries of the small Missouri town where he first set up shop. W.I. (man at right) is pictured here (in the 1950s) with his grandchildren Anne Westlake Elsberry and Doug Burton, who grew up to see Westlake Hardware become one of the most successful hardware chains in the Midwest.

Foreward Message

> ### Remember, we are LEADERS in all kinds of Hardware, Stoves and Ranges....
> —Westlake & Doyle advertisement on July 19, 1907

Howard Elsberry

Westlake Hardware
President
Chief Executive Officer
Chairman of the Board

W.I. had only been in the hardware business two years when he made this statement that still echoes within the Westlake organization:

Remember, we are LEADERS...

The "Old-Timers" within the organization know that F.K. Westlake always remembered. His goal for the Westlake organization was simple: To have the best hardware stores in the country.

To reach that goal, he not only reorganized, remerchandised, and relocated stores, he also searched out LEADERS to catch his vision and expand it. He recruited some of these leaders from outside the company. Others, he found within Westlake. "I want a partner," he would tell them. And, in 1972, Westlake Ace Hardware was recognized as the best hardware retailer in the country.

Remember, we are LEADERS...

At Westlake, we still search for leaders and partners. We've fine tuned our goal: To be the best neighborhood hardware store in the market. At 100 years old, we're still growing. We're still innovators. We're still agile enough to change quickly. Our vision is still focused on the customer and what we can do to serve them best. We look forward to change and new opportunities. We don't look back at what worked yesterday. We look for what will be needed tomorrow.

However, this is our 100th anniversary. It's a time to pause, look back, and reflect on the events and people that have made Westlake the best. Our history includes some truly amazing people who saw opportunities no one else saw and who built a legacy that we all enjoy today. They deserve to be remembered. They deserve our respect. We're grateful to them. We're also grateful for our vendors who have partnered with us in making Westlake a success for 100 years—and for helping us commemorate that success in this book.

We're especially grateful to our neighbors and customers. Thank you for the privilege of serving you for the past 100 years. We promise you that we will remember the truest definition of leadership is "service." Service to our customers. Service to our communities. We will remember and we will continue to serve.

So, please take a few moments and enjoy this history. Think about the challenges that Westlake has already overcome. If you are a Westlake associate, congratulate yourself on being a part of this story. Just know this: If W.I., Miss Scottie, F.K. and all the Westlake associates over the past 100 years could ask just one thing of the Westlake associates and management who carry on their tradition, it would be this:

Remember, we are LEADERS...

Howard Elsberry
President and CEO

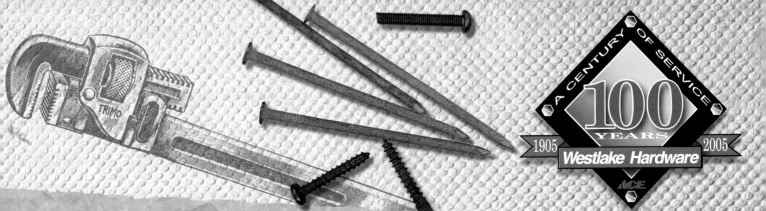

The First Generation

Westlake's first store--
Huntsville, Missouri

"We will sell you GOOD GOODS and GUARANTEE them"

The original Huntsville, Missouri, hardware store (Doyle and Bagby) as it might have looked when W.I. Westlake was hired, ca. 1905.

The First Generation

He'd met his match

W.I. and Scottie Westlake posed for this portrait on their wedding day in 1905.

In 1905 William Irvin Westlake—"Irvin" to his mom, "W.I." to friends—turned 30. At the time, he was a bachelor working as a clerk in the Thurston Hardware Store in Clifton Hill, Missouri. As befits a man of that age in that era, he decided the moment was right to get serious about life.

A short time before, he had gone to a small party at a farmhouse just south of Clifton Hill. There he spied an attractive young woman with flaming red hair. "I'd sit down next to you," he said, feeling his oats, "but I'm afraid I'd catch on fire."

"Don't worry," replied the girl, Scottie Knox by name, the farmer's daughter, "you're too green to burn." W.I. had to smile. He had met his match, and he knew it. He proposed a short time later.

In April, W.I. resigned his position at Thurston's and left for nearby Huntsville to enter the employ of Messrs. Bagby and Doyle, "hardware merchants of that place." This change in employment was significant enough to merit newspaper coverage. "Mr. Westlake is one of the best young men in the county, a splendid businessman," observed the *Huntsville Herald*, "and Doyle and Bagby can congratulate themselves on securing his service."

Less than a month later, the first Westlake & Doyle ad ran in the local newspaper. It turns out that W.I. had not just gone to work for Messrs. Bagby and Doyle. With the help of Scottie and her parents, he had actually purchased the Bagby interest in the store. On November 29 of that same year, W.I. married the lovely—and sassy—young Scottie. She had just turned 22. The newlyweds made their home in Huntsville.

This had to be an exciting move for W.I. and Scottie. Clifton Hill—like so many small towns across the country—had its own hardware store, dry goods store, post office, and weekly newspaper. But Huntsville was the Randolph County seat, a city of about 2,000 people—much larger than Clifton Hill.

Okay, maybe Moberly, six miles to the east, had surpassed Huntsville in population. Moberly didn't come into existence until the railroads crossed there just 40 years earlier. From that moment on, the town sprang up from the countryside as if by magic, thus earning the nickname "The Magic City." By 1905, Moberly had more than 9,000 people, easily the most in Randolph County.

But, as the St. Louis papers were quick to point out, Moberly also had the crime and vice you would expect from a railroad boomtown and little of the sophistication and culture of the more stately Huntsville. And if those upstarts from Moberly thought they could wrest the county seat away from Huntsville, they had another think coming.

Humble beginnings

This photo shows the interior of the first Westlake's store in Huntsville, Missouri, ca. 1930. It shows Westlake's merchandise and staff about 20 years after W.I. Westlake bought into his share of the store.

W.I. Westlake

The founder of Westlake is shown in this detail of the photo above.

Tales around the stove

As W.I. soon learned, when the families came to town on Saturday by horse and buggy, the men would congregate around the hardware store's pot-bellied stove. There, the stories would fly as fast as the tobacco juice, but with not near the accuracy.

From these folks' perspective, the world seemed to be turning much more quickly than ours does. By 1905, a watershed moment in the history of invention, the big Missouri cities had absorbed a stunning new array of technology. While little of this technology had made its way to mid-state, everyone had at least heard about all the newfangled inventions. The cities—at least, their hotels, their businesses, and fancier homes—had electricity, telephones, central heating, and indoor plumbing. In 1905, typically, the smaller towns had none of the above.

However, one invention had already begun to reshape mid-America. In 1880, just 25 years before, the first liquid fuel tractor had been invented. The effect of the tractor was to make farming much less labor intensive. Farms grew larger, but the farm population grew smaller. In fact, the farm population of Missouri would peak in 1900 and decline slowly thereafter. Many of the children who had grown up on farms—like W.I. and Scottie—made their way to the small towns and cities throughout the Midwest and beyond to find their fortunes.

To maintain the rural tradition of self-reliance, however, small town Americans needed two essential things: the first was tools and the second, as W.I. understood from the beginning, was advice.

The pace of progress

Although Einstein discovered the theory of relativity in 1905, life in Huntsville was moving at something less than the speed of light. The horse still powered their world, and the sale of horse-related gear drove sales at the hardware store: horse collars, saddles, bridles, you name it. The store would continue to sell these items for almost the next 50 years.

When the Westlakes moved to Huntsville, an automobile sighting was something of an event. True, the Duryea brothers had manufactured the first practical American automobiles ten years earlier, and some had already shown up on the streets of Kansas City and St. Louis, but there were precious few in between.

To say the least, the infrastructure wasn't quite ready to support the motorcar. It would be three more years before Henry Ford produced his first Model T and turned America into a country of automobiles.

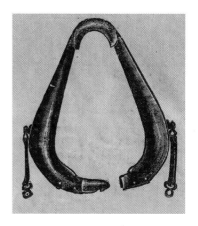

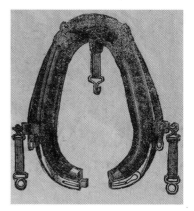

Outwitting the outlaws

The diamond in this ring is the one Scottie saved from the robbers. It was originally in a Tiffany setting; Anne had it reset into this striking design.

When the young Westlake couple settled in Huntsville, Scottie commuted the eight miles back to the family's Clifton Hill dry goods store—by train.

With the death of Jesse James twenty-some years earlier, Missouri had shed its reputation as the "outlaw state," but no one had told the outlaws. On one of Scottie's early work commutes, a gang of desperados boarded the train and commenced to separate the passengers from their valuables. The quick-thinking Scottie turned the one-carat diamond she was sporting inwards and passed it off as a wedding ring—which the thieves let her keep. Many years later she would give that ring to Anne Elsberry, her granddaughter and now Westlake's General Counsel.

Exception to the norm

Scottie was always a little smarter and more ambitious than the average farmer's daughter, qualities that have passed on down through the generations. She had attended college. There weren't many women in Missouri who could say the same, or men either. That college is now known as Central Methodist University, a college to which her family has donated generously. The stately Cross Memorial Tower on campus bears witness to the same. Scottie put that education to work, first at the Clifton Hill dry goods store, then at managing several stores of her own in Huntsville. She would be acknowledged as one of the most influential business leaders in Huntsville.

The Cross Memorial Tower on the campus of Central Methodist University, located in Fayette, Missouri. The tower was named after Scottie's mother's first cousin, J.T. Cross of J.T. Cross Lumber in Moberly, Missouri.

The quadrangle of Central Methodist University as it looked in 1929.

Huntsville—
Main Street U.S.A.

*An early postcard
shows Depot Street
in Huntsville, much
as it would have
looked when W.I.
entered the
hardware business.*

Photo courtesy of the Huntsville Historical Society, Huntsville, Missouri

A Midwestern whistle stop

*Scottie Westlake would have been very familiar with the Huntsville
railroad depot as she traveled back and forth to Clifton Hill.*

Competitive juices

Those who romanticize a more cooperative, less competitive past in the hardware business obviously were not in Huntsville a hundred years ago. The day that Doyle & Bagby announced its hiring of W.I. Westlake, Thorne and Key—"The Hardware Men" of Moberly—ran a large display ad square in the Huntsville paper offering ice cream freezers, lawn mowers, windows, and door screens for sale. They also promised "fair, open dealing" in a "clean, light store."

When W.I. became a partner in the business, the very first ad he and Doyle ran featured a cooking exhibit on one of the Never Break ranges they offered. Better yet, they promised coffee and biscuits "free to all."

If today, small town merchants worry about the Internet and so-called "big boxes," a century ago they also faced a variety of new commercial challenges. An ad in the *Huntsville Herald* from 1907 warned about one of them, the threat posed by local people "mailing their money to the big city for Mail Order bargains."

The likely consequences to small town America of the mail order incursion were ominous if a bit overblown. "Home merchants don't thrive," read the ad, "grass grows in the streets, no jobs are to be had, no opening for a new business, and the young man goes to the city."

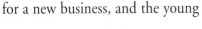
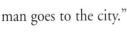

> # Do You Love Your Wife?
>
> She wants a refrigerator and you can buy one while they last for less than cost. Gasoline stoves for $2 and up. Lawn mowers and screening wire at your own price.
>
> All the leading makers of cooking stoves and ranges we are offering at prices to meet all competition.
>
> We have in stock an excellent line of pocket knives, razors and shears and in fact a full line of all kinds of hardware that we are selling at prices that will make friends of our customers. We want your trade and will sell you GOOD GOODS and GUARANTEE them to give satisfaction. We invite you to come in and get prices.
>
> ## Westlake & Doyle Hdw. Co.

In Huntsville, W.I.'s principal early competitor was W.S. Thomas ("The Hardware Man"). Although most of a hardware store's customers were men—and most of Thomas's ads were written to appeal to them—Thomas also competed for the female trade with price point advertising: an extra strong egg beater for 8¢, an ice chipper for 9¢, a potato slicer for 25¢, and Mrs. Potts' famed iron set for just 90¢.

Westlake and Doyle on the other hand played the psychology card, and they did so with surprising sophistication. "Do You Love Your Wife?" asked the headline of an early ad. "She wants a refrigerator," the copy continued, "and you can buy one while they last for less than cost." These savvy merchants also offered cooking stoves and ranges but were not about to ignore their male customer base, tempting them with "an excellent line" of pocket knives, razors, and shears at prices that promised to make "friends of our customers."

Early on, the partners embarked on a strategy to increase market share and did not shy from explaining that strategy to the public. "Small Profits, More Customers, is Our Motto," read the subhead of a large display ad. However low the price, however friendly the service, they did expect their customers to pay their bills.

"Have you resolved to pay Westlake & Doyle the balance you owe them on 1906 account?" asked the pair in a New Year's ad of 1907. "Save us the trouble of looking for you or sending you a DUN."

The Midwest work ethic

In January 1908, W.I. took his next major step on the road to responsibility when he purchased Doyle's half of the business and changed the name of the store to W.I. Westlake's Hardware Store. Later, the store's name would appear in ads simply as "W.I. Westlake."

Westlake was never just about hardware. It was always about "software" as well—the early and ongoing software of patient, instructive service. In fact, the first ad W.I. ran as sole proprietor featured a Grand Standard Sewing Machine. What made the ad particularly intriguing was that it invited customers to come and see the machine "in operation by an expert sewer." Indicative of the time and place, this ad, like most early ads, did not list a phone number or even an address. People simply knew.

Having grown up on a farm like most everyone else in Huntsville, W.I. brought the rural values to the store with him each morning. He worked hard. He worked honestly. He worked long hours. He worked independently. And, important for the proprietor of a hardware store, he knew how just about everything worked.

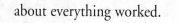

The Westlake children

*F.K. and his younger
sister, Martha Will.*

Family values

W.I. focused his loving attention on his growing family, on a nearby farm
he purchased, and on his 23 ft. by 80 ft. store, a fairly typical size back then.
On Valentine's Day in 1915, Scottie Westlake gave birth to the couple's first
child, Francis Knox Westlake, better known as F.K. or Frank. Eight years later,
daughter Martha Will was born.

The kids loved the shop and made it their home away from home. As
Martha Will came of age she and F.K. would help out as best they could, doing,
she remembers, everything there was to do. Meanwhile, Scottie continued to
work in a mercantile store, now in Huntsville.

Except for Sunday, then still honored as a day of rest, the family rarely
stopped working. Martha Will remembers her father getting to the store early
every morning to take care of the coal miners before they left for the nearby

Handwritten on image: Huntsville Coal Mine

Westlake's was a stop on the way to work

This image from a 1907 postcard shows one of the many mines in the area.

mines. One product the store moved great quantities of was Canned Heat. Despite its name, the product's main benefit was light, not warmth. The miners would use it to fuel their "pit lamps," the open lamps worn on their caps. (Later, carbide would become the preferred fuel.) "We sold so much of it," Martha Will recalls, "that my father wondered whether the miners might be drinking it."

W.I. set the mold for the kind of worker the company looks for even today: one with a superior work ethic, strong family values, upstanding character, and a commitment to the community. W.I. joined the Rotary Club as a charter member, was elected to the school board, and served on the board of the First Methodist Church—including a stretch as chairman. W.I. also served for several years as president of the Farmer and Merchant's Bank of Huntsville.

Bank president or not, W.I. had his own personal ethic about money. What everyone remembers is that if someone needed financial help, no questions asked, they went not to the bank but to W.I. "He loaned money to everybody who came and asked for it," remembers Martha Will. Nor did he charge interest.

Memories to last a lifetime

Martha Will's son, Doug Burton, now Executive Vice President of Westlake, remembers W.I. from a unique perspective. Doug's father died when he was just seventeen months old. For the next several years, he lived with his grandparents just a few blocks from the Huntsville store. On many occasions, W.I. would look after Doug at the store, giving him a hammer and nails and setting him loose. Doug remembers one time when a customer spotted him hammering nails into the floor in the back of the store and promptly informed W.I. "Boy's gotta do somethin'," replied W.I., unperturbed. "Other people called him W.I.," recalls Doug. "I called him Dad. I thought the world of him."

From his small boy's perspective, Doug was drawn to the rolling ladders that stretched to the ceiling and allowed W.I. and his staff to retrieve the hundreds of separate items that sat in open bins along the walls. The store also sold seed from open bins. Martha Will has a particularly fond memory of being allowed to measure it out for the customers. Both keenly remember the pot-bellied stove that served as the store's heart for the 50 years of its existence. On Saturday nights in particular, men from the area would sit around that stove and swap stories well past midnight; this they were doing in 1950, just as they had done in 1905.

**Doug Burton
in his younger days**

A whiff of ambition

W.I. Westlake

By 1927, the senior Westlake had served his company well. Although he would remain active in the business, he began grooming his son F.K. to take over the reins.

The young F.K. absorbed much of his father's character and work ethic. By age 12 in fact, the industrious boy would manage the store when W.I. would leave to work the farm. As he grew older he took on more and more responsibility, including dynamite runs to the coal mines in his father's Model A.

His ambition and sense of destiny, however, was another thing. These were epidemic during America's Roaring Twenties. 1927, the same year F.K. started managing the store, stands out. Another small town lad had managed to convince a group of Missouri businessmen to fund his proposed venture. To honor their home town, he christened their investment "The Spirit of St. Louis." In May of that year, 25-year-old Charles Lindbergh's solitary crossing of the Atlantic enlarged the dreams of every young boy in the nation—F.K.'s included.

Two years later the stock market crashed, the Depression followed, and many of those dreams were put on hold, the Westlakes' among them. The Westlakes did not, however, abandon their dreams, their store, or their commitment to their community. As best he could, W.I. continued to lend money to those neighbors who needed it, and the good souls of Huntsville soldiered on.

A study in contrasts

The Roaring Twenties was a time of great prosperity and peace, culminating in devastating poverty. The optimism of the early part of the decade virtually vanished in October 1929 as the stock market plummeted. Westlake's "weathered the storm" in the early 1930s.

A typical Midwestern hardware store

This photograph, location identified as Moberly, ca. 1930, is believed to show the interior of the downtown Moberly store that F.K. Westlake eventually acquired. Moberly became F.K.'s home, and headquarters for Westlake Hardware in the 1950s.

WESTLAKE'S
ACE HARDWARE

A CENTURY OF SERVICE
100 YEARS
1905 — 2005
Westlake Hardware
ACE

The Second Generation

Missouri's seat of higher education

The University of Missouri in Columbia, Missouri, has graduated many members of the Westlake organization. Centrally located in the state and in the country, it plays a vital role in educating future generations.

F.K. Westlake saved enough money clerking in the store on weekends and after school to make college a reality. In 1932—in the bleak stretch of the Depression—the always-optimistic F.K. graduated as valedictorian of his high school class and headed off to the University of Missouri in nearby Columbia. At that time, not many more people were going to college than in Scottie's days. F.K., a Phi Beta Kappa, graduated from MU's School of Business and Public Administration in 1936.

In his own retelling, F.K. Westlake headed to St. Louis after graduation to try his hand as a stockbroker. His sister Martha Will also remembers him going to Galesburg, Illinois, to get his foot in the door of the shoe business. In either case, his timing was less than spectacular. As old-timers will tell you, the recession of 1937–1938 may have been the gloomiest period of the Great Depression. Whether F.K. was selling stocks or shoes, he wasn't going to sell much of either.

F.K. Westlake

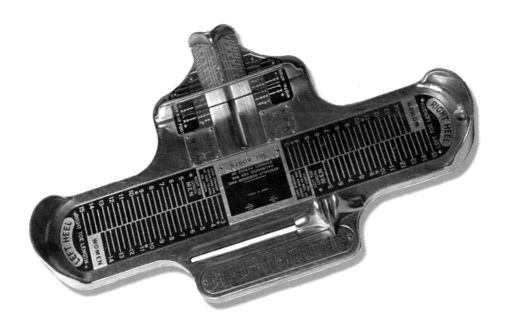

Back to the basics

Returning to what he knew best, in April 1938 F.K. bought a small hardware store in Shelbina, Missouri, a town of roughly 2,000 people about 55 miles northeast of Huntsville. The *Shelbina Democrat* reported the event, but, as one might expect, with no sense of its historical import. "After 39 years as a Shelbina merchant," read the brief account, "John C. Jewett has sold his hardware store to F.K. Westlake of Huntsville, giving possession Monday."

As F.K. understood, the population of this town had peaked 25 years earlier. This 2,500 square foot hardware store—about the same size as his father's—was not to be the end of the line for him but rather the beginning.

Brand identity

Co-op advertising has always been a popular method of getting the word out to the public—especially in hardware. Both entities benefited from this metal sign, meant to be nailed to the side of a building.

Opportunity knocks

The same day that the paper announced F.K.'s arrival in Shelbina, he ran a display ad for the new "Westlake Hardware Company." Among the items listed were Coleman Stoves. Soon after F.K. set up shop, he met the salesman for the company that sold those stoves, a personable young fellow named Kenneth (Kenny) Dickson.

Both F.K. and Kenny were young, ambitious, and talented. No one knows which of the two first came up with the idea of creating their own business. They both wanted something they could own, something they could manage themselves, and something with a future. They found that future in propane.

"The Coleman stove used fuel oil. Propane was just coming of age," says Kenny's son, Bill Dickson, a shareholder and member of Westlake's Board of Directors. "It was a natural segue from Coleman into propane."

In 1941, the young partners had just about everything they needed to start a new enterprise: a solid idea, sound business acumen, a good work ethic, a world of ambition, and a smart new name—Uregas Service, Incorporated. The only thing they didn't have was money. For that, they turned to the one man who they knew would not turn them down—W.I., who never turned down a request for a loan.

"It is not your gas," W.I. would joke with F.K. and Kenny. "It's our gas." The 66-year-old W.I. was named president when the company incorporated in April 1941. Kenny Dickson was made vice president and general manager and F.K. was named treasurer. They chose Moberly, easily the largest and most strategically located city in Randolph County, to be the home of its first small office and bulk plant.

Getting your name out there

Providing a continual reminder of your firm's name is the reason for specialty advertising. Giveaways such as yardsticks and calendars reminded customers where to go for goods and services.

A greater challenge

Kenny Dickson

1941 was a busy year for F.K. Westlake. Not only did he start a business, but he also married the lovely young Virginia Morgan. Just as F.K. was adjusting to married life and the company was about to get up and running, fate intervened in a major way. Army reservist F.K. Westlake was called into service as a first lieutenant, infantry, the United States Army. This was in October 1941. Two months later, with the bombing of Pearl Harbor, F.K. and his partners realized that he might not be back in the very near future.

His son Bill points out that Kenny Dickson's "bum knee" was the company's good fortune. Because Kenny was classified 4-F, he was able to stay and guide the new company. The son of a Methodist minister, Kenny had not been able to afford college, but he worked hard and, according to Bill, had "managerial qualities. He made something of himself. He could get people to do what he wanted them to do. He always tried to be fair," remembers Bill. "Fair and hard-working. If you say that, you've described my father."

With Kenny in charge of Uregas, F.K. still had to find someone to take care of his hardware store while he was gone. He chose Alva Bagley, an older gentleman who would not be called to serve. Alva had been working at the Purdin Mercantile Company, a department store in Purdin, Missouri, before F.K. recruited him.

Serving the country... overseas and at home

While still at the department store, Alva had hired a recent graduate from Purdin High School. Alva was hoping to groom this young man to follow in his footsteps, but Uncle Sam wanted Ben Barrows too.

It is still a mystery to Ben how a farm boy with a weak stomach from the middle of the country found his way into the Coast Guard, but once there he made the best of it. In the Coast Guard he served on an Amphibious Attack Transport (APA-13) and participated in the invasions of North Africa, Sicily, and Italy. Under pressure, Ben will even admit that, yes, on June 6, 1944, he manned the transport's battle station as the ship made two separate trips to the Normandy coast. "It wasn't as rough on the Navy as the Army," Ben quickly adds, lest one think he did anything memorable or even difficult.

Ben was transferred to shore duty in 1945. As soon as it was certain he would not be sent back to sea, his fiancée Lorene came to New Jersey where he was stationed. They were married there in New Jersey, but were already planning to go back home to Missouri. Ben had accepted Bagley's offer to work with him at F.K. Westlake's Shelbina store as a clerk. In taking that job, Ben began a 60-year relationship with Westlake Hardware that continues to this day.

Ben Barrows
This photo was taken during WWII, when Ben served in the Coast Guard.

Back to business

In the years immediately after the war, the stores specialized in two items above all. One, not surprisingly, was Uregas. The second was appliances. For the first time in four years, America's appliance companies could make something other than war materials. And America's young people were getting married, having children, and demanding major household appliances as they never had before. As a result, appliances filled about every square foot of floor space in the small hardware stores.

Ben remembers opening a new Westlake Hardware store in Monroe City in 1946 as an assistant manager. So hard to get was some of the merchandise that when people came in on the Grand Opening Day they dropped their names in a box to see who would be chosen for a chance to buy a refrigerator or a washing machine.

The latest "must-have" conveniences

As Westlake's Hardware began its expansion to nearby towns, all stores continued to thrive by stocking popular appliances as well as hardware. Myrmell Smith, an employee of the Monroe City store, is posing with the time-saving appliances.

Making a mark in Moberly

The first Westlake store in Moberly opened in 1949. The store was moved to this larger location in 1955.

In 1949, F.K. Westlake and Kenny Dickson turned their attention back to hardware. In that year, they incorporated the Westlake Hardware Company and opened a new store in Moberly, the headquarters for Uregas. This was their first hardware store in "The Magic City." It was in Moberly, too, that Westlake Hardware would be headquartered for the next generation and where F.K. Westlake would raise his family.

REED STREET, LOOKING EAST FROM 4TH ST., MOBERLY, MO.

UNION STATION, MOBERLY, MO.

"The Magic City"

These postcards from the 1920s show the bustling atmosphere of downtown Moberly, Missouri. The Union Station was a vital part of the economic boost Moberly gained from the railroad industry.

Their reinvestment in hardware was well timed. If 1900 marked the year that the farm population began to decline, the 1940s saw that decline accelerate as it never had before. One reason, of course, was the war. Another cause, one that would continue to improve rural life, was electrification. But the bottom line remained the tractor. At the start of the war, 30 million people lived on farms with 1.2 million tractors. By 1950, the number of tractors had climbed to almost 4 million, and the number of people on farms had fallen to 23 million.

Rural people were joining their fellow Americans in the small towns and now burgeoning suburbs of the Midwest. They would provide a good percentage of the customer base for Westlake Hardware and even higher percentage of its staff, especially in the early years. At Westlake Hardware, farm kids who knew how to fix most everything could share their knowledge with a customer base that would need more and more help.

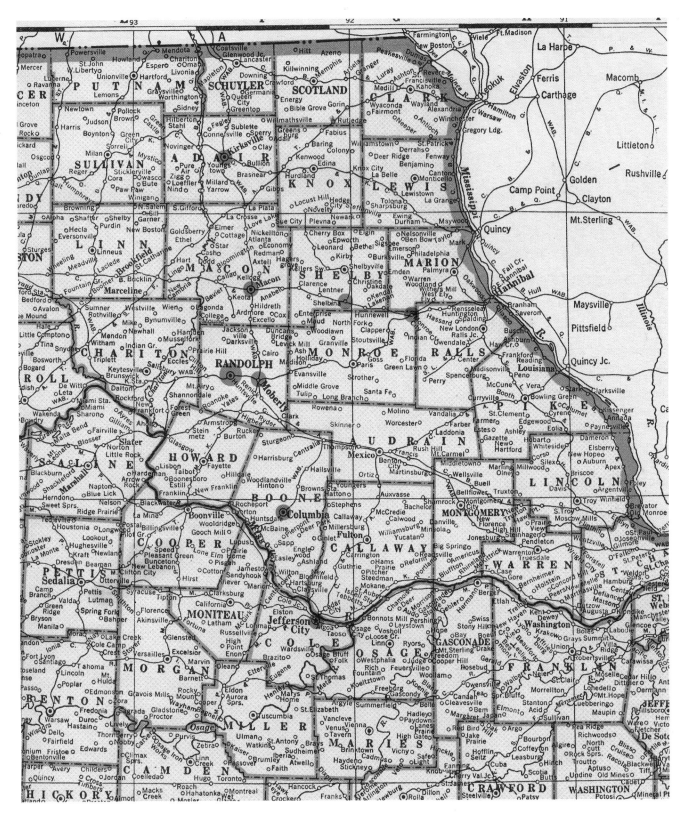

Outward expansion

Beginning with the original Huntsville location, the Westlake operation grew to include Shelbina, Monroe City and Moberly (shown in pink). As the 1960s took hold, F.K. and his manager-partners acquired locations in Macon, Columbia, Kirksville, and Jefferson City (shown in purple).

The self-service revolution

The men who worked with him always claimed that, no matter what other businesses he was involved in, F.K.'s first love was the hardware business. In 1955, F.K. bought the Newman Hardware Store in downtown Moberly. He planned to move his own hardware store to that location, consolidate the two stores, and try something entirely new. In announcing the move, Westlake promised the new store "would be one of the most complete and modern in this section of Missouri."

F.K. went to work immediately on the Newman building, adding a new front, improving the lighting, laying new floors, and even putting in air conditioning—then still a novelty. What is more, F.K. had an inspiration, one that he had gleaned at a brand new kind of grocery store called a "supermarket." In 1955, almost all hardware stores still had the long counters and rolling ladders. The customers would tell the clerk what they wanted; the clerk would climb the ladders, retrieve the item and then ring up the sale.

The new Westlake store in Moberly had open displays for easy self-selection. For the first time, customers could actually browse through the merchandise themselves, select their own items and take them to the cash registers. Even though customers could serve themselves, the Moberly store retained the sense of partnership between the buyer and the seller in the fulfillment of the buyer's dreams, the things he would do himself with the advice of the knowledgeable store clerk.

"We tried something unheard of in the hardware business—self service," F.K. Westlake recalled in a 1984 interview, "and the concept worked." The year was 1955, the 50th anniversary of Westlake Hardware and something of a new beginning.

Supermarket for hardware

The interior of the downtown Moberly store was brightly lit, offering air conditioning and clearly marked aisles. The self-service concept allowed customers to "help themselves"— a concept that worked perfectly with Westlake's merchandising.

New worlds to conquer

The self-service concept worked so well, in fact, that F.K. Westlake looked around for new worlds to conquer. He found one in Columbia, the growing home of the University of Missouri and the largest city in mid-Missouri. By 1959, in fact, Columbia had more than 35,000 people, twice as many as it had just 20 years earlier.

"Frank was able to see the potential of a location," observed Paul Kuckelman, the manager of the first Columbia store. "He just eyeballed it." Paul was not the only one to make this observation, and there is no denying the value of the gift. But F.K.'s real gift, an uncanny one, one that Paul and others were too modest to call attention to, was F.K.'s ability to spot the potential in people.

Ben Barrows was already a valued contributor to the Westlake organization. Starting with Paul Kuckelman, F.K. Westlake would hire three more key manager-partners in the first five years of the "self-service revolution." These four would stay with Westlake a minimum of 40 years each. Together, they formed a core that would strengthen Westlake, shepherd it through adversity, and see it prosper into the 21st century.

"He (F.K.) just eyeballed it."

(Left) *In 1959, F.K. Westlake spotted this location for his new Columbia store—then occupied by a large brick house.*

(Bottom) *The Knipp Construction Company in Columbia, Missouri, was so proud of constructing the new Westlake's building, it took out a half-page newspaper ad touting the fact when it was finished in September.*

Paul Kuckelman graduated from Kansas State University in 1949 and drifted into retail because that's where the jobs were. It did not take him long to realize that he wanted to be his own boss. After working ten years in Kansas City, he explored the possibility of buying or managing a variety store. One of his contacts knew F.K. and knew he was looking for someone to run a store. He put the two in contact and F.K. interviewed Paul in Kansas City. Both of the men obviously liked what they saw. The two then inspected the site in Columbia, favored it, and along with Kenny, formed a three-person partnership to build and manage a store. Said Paul in a 2001 interview, "The rest is history."

F.K. Westlake had chosen well. "Paul Kuckelman was legendary for a strong work ethic," observes Anne Elsberry. She makes a compelling case that it was Paul who set the Westlake standard for hard and conscientious work, a standard that other managers have strived to honor.

The partners opened the Columbia store in September 1959. The rollout was impressive. The partners unveiled this "splendid new building" after an escalating series of promotions. These culminated in the Grand Opening, three days of "dollar day" sales. With "free parking and plenty of it," this store promised to be "Columbia's most modern self service shopping convenience" and it delivered.

This store was also the prototype for the stores to follow. F.K. Westlake reasoned that self service and an upfront checkout would work with the right layout, and it did. "Customers seemed to like our system," said Paul, and the store proved "very profitable" from the start.

One of the "Big Four"

Paul Kuckelman poses next to an extensive display of bolts, rivets, screws, washers, wing nuts, and the like offered in the well-stocked Columbia store, ca. 1962.

Building the anticipation

During construction, a huge sign covering the windows of the new Columbia store created a buzz of excitement in the community.

Columbia gets its second Westlake's

This aerial view from 1965 shows the latest addition to the hardware scene—at 32,000 square feet, it was a borderline tourist attraction.

At the time, and for many years to come, each store was a separate corporation. From the beginning, too, managers in the Westlake family were given a great deal of freedom to experiment, and Paul did just that. Some experiments worked very well, like the sale of lumber at the Columbia store. Others, like a Tiki Hut with exotic gifts, admitted Paul with a wry smile, didn't work. Enough experiments worked well enough that F.K. Westlake and Paul Kuckelman opened a second huge, new, cutting-edge Columbia store in 1965.

Ace is the place

1959 proved to be a milestone year not only in the way Westlake Hardware sold its merchandise, but also in the way the company bought it. Historically, "jobbers" would come to the stores with their catalogues, and the store managers would buy supplies through these middleman. This was a relatively slow, cumbersome and uncertain process. As Westlake Hardware expanded, F.K. Westlake realized that he would need a new supply system to succeed. F.K. began reviewing his options in a fashion that Paul Kuckelman

A partnership built to last
Dealing directly with Chicago-based supplier Ace Hardware saved time and expense.

described as "very thorough, very analytical, and very practical." His final decision was that a partnership with Ace would be a "real good thing."

F.K. liked how the Chicago-based Ace Hardware company did business. The company had formed 35 years before when four Chicago-area hardware owners decided they could increase their buying power if they bought cooperatively. Within five years, they had expanded their co-op to 11 stores and

Signs of the times

The Ace name became an important component to the Westlake identity as shown in the exterior signage for these two stores (right: Lawrence, Kansas; bottom: Omaha, Nebraska).

Westlake's Ace Hardware
This logo appeared in newspaper advertising from 1959 to the 1980s.

built their first warehouse, a 25,000 square foot facility in Chicago. The company rode through the Depression and the war, continuing to add new members as it went. By 1959, there were nearly 300 stores in the Ace family.

"Some people talk about dedication," said Art Krausman, president and general manager at the time of Ace's 50th anniversary. "Ace's founders lived it." In the same interview, he recalled that "Everything was done to keep costs down." Ace bought second-hand furniture and equipment, painted their walls in outdated colors and even saved paper clips to use again.

Although F.K. was interested in a partnership, Dick Hesse, president of Ace Hardware, was hesitant. Dick Hesse, one of the founders of Ace Hardware is remembered as a "colorful, controversial president, a dynamic and determined ex-hardware retailer" who was totally and completely dedicated to Ace's success. He was not sure that Ace could service a store as far away as the Westlake stores were, at least 300 miles from Chicago. F.K. was confident the partnership could work and he sold Ace on the plan. Today, the question seems academic as Ace has stores in 62 countries and all 50 states, but it was not academic then. The Moberly Westlake store came on line as Ace store 297. The Columbia Westlake store was 298. In fact, the Columbia store was promoted as "Westlake's Ace Hardware." Although Ace has more than 5,000 stores today, Westlake Hardware remains its largest volume dealer.

"The relationship has stood the test of time," said Paul Kuckelman more than 40 years after it began, "and just improved."

W.I. and Scottie celebrate 50 years together

A family portrait was taken in 1955, when the Westlakes marked their golden anniversary. Behind Scottie and W.I. are son-in-law Nathan Casto and daughter Martha Will Casto with grandson Doug Burton. Beside Doug is granddaughter Anne Westlake (Elsberry) with her mother and father, Virginia and F.K. Westlake.

Changing of the guard

Not all the Westlake milestones in 1959 were causes for celebration. After 54 years of hard honest labor, W.I. Westlake died at the age of 84. He worked nearly to the end in his Huntsville store and enjoyed every day of it, a sense of joy he passed on to his son. As F.K. would say of the hardware business, "If you can't have fun, get out of it." By all accounts, F.K., like W.I. before him, savored the small pleasures the job held and never hesitated to share them.

Like Paul Kuckelman, Al Hall was restless. Having worked 17 years with the Woolworth Company and weary of the constant travel, Al wanted something close to home where he could hang his hat and feel good about it. "I was looking for something I could own," he admits.

Al had a friend in Moberly who introduced him to a mutual friend, F.K. Westlake. F.K. encouraged Al to visit Paul Kuckelman in his new store in Columbia. Al did and liked what he saw. In their next meeting, F.K. told Al that he had his eyes on Jefferson City and would contact him when the right opportunity came along. F.K. explained to Al that he believed it would take at least three months and maybe a year before the right site came available.

Three days later Al picked up the phone, and he could not have been more surprised if Harry Truman had called him. It was F.K. Westlake. He asked Al if he was ready to take the plunge. F.K.'s number one site had suddenly become available. "I don't want a manager," F.K. added, "I want a partner."

When the two toured the weed-infested site, Al was incredulous. "This is going to be a hardware store?" he asked. Yes, it was. F.K., remember, had a gift for finding sites. Together, they opened the Jefferson City store in November 1961, the third Westlake store in the Ace family. At 11,000 square feet, it was

Al Hall
This photo of Al dates from the 1970s.

A "Capitol" location

The Jefferson City, Missouri, store was yet another successful location for the Westlake chain.

the biggest in the growing Westlake family. "We weren't sure how we'd fill all that space," F.K. recalled, "but we managed somehow." They would relocate the store in an even larger location ten years later.

Seeing the potential in Jefferson City, F.K. offered the assistant manager job to a young fellow with potential named Wade Coorts. A country boy, Wade had gotten to know Moberly—and Moberly him—when he played basketball at Moberly Junior College. After a stint in the Army and a job with an oil company that kept him on the road too much, Wade had taken a job at the Moberly Westlake in 1960 as a department buyer.

"We hit it off from the start," says Wade of F.K. Westlake. "He was always a great person to work for, a good man to guide you in the right direction." In Jefferson City, he learned a lot from Al Hall as well. His career with Westlake was just beginning.

Expansion becomes a necessity

Shortly after acquiring the Jefferson City location, it soon became obvious that Westlake's could fill yet another niche—that of lumber and building materials supplier. The "Lumberteria" addition (above) offered the citizens of Jefferson City a wide selection of lumber and building products.

The Jefferson City store was relocated in the 1970s to its present address (below). The bright red accents to the exterior and bold signage can't be missed by travelers on the busy highway located in front of the store.

Throughout the 1950s, the Uregas Company, which F.K. had started with his father and Kenny Dickson, had been flourishing. By the 1960s the company, still headquartered in Moberly, had more than 200 employees and nearly 100,000 customers. It was the largest privately-owned propane business in the country, Bill Dickson recalls, and so prominent that an east-coast propane business was actively recruiting Kenny Dickson for their CEO position.

Although Kenny chose to remain with Uregas, something—perhaps the recruiting effort, perhaps W.I.'s death, perhaps an awareness that they were at the peak of their business—prompted F.K. and Kenny to reconsider their businesses. While the partners always consulted each other on major decisions, neither "tampered with" the day to day operations of the other's business. Kenny was in charge of the daily operations of Uregas; F.K. was in charge of the daily operations of Westlake Hardware.

In 1962, F.K. sold his interest in Uregas and Kenny Dickson merged the company with Suburban Gas Company of Pomona, California. Kenny kept his interest in the merged Uregas companies and stayed on as president until he sold his interest in 1963.

It was not until the Uregas sale that Bill Dickson remembers any lawyers being involved in the partnership. By this time, F.K. and Kenny had been partners for more than 20 years. They would stay partners for nearly 30 years more.

Just the beginning

Ben Barrows poses in front of the Monroe City store, where he had been manager for 18 years. In 1962, he would make the move to Macon, Missouri.

"It's beginning to look a lot like Christmas..."

What downtown store would be complete without displays for the window-shoppers? The Monroe City shop window was festively decorated with a then-popular aluminum Christmas tree.

In 1962, change was in store for Ben Barrows as well. Ben had been managing a 2,500 square foot Westlake Hardware store in Monroe City since 1946, when F.K. Westlake decided it was time to move to a bigger town. He had Macon in mind, a city of more than 5,000 people and twice the size of Monroe City.

In 1962 F.K. spied a store there that he liked. "We're going to offer so many dollars," F.K. told Ben. "The owner will pick up his personal things, and we'll take over." That's exactly what happened. F.K. made an offer. The owner accepted, cleared out the cash register and left everything behind for the new owners, including his employees.

"Frank was sharp about those sort of things," remembers Ben fondly. F.K. and Ben moved right in with Ben now as a partner. They put their own money in the cash register, kept the same employees, and sold off the merchandise they didn't like.

Moving up in Macon

This larger building, located across the street from the former store, provided more room and storage for the Macon business. However, this location also proved too small for the growing Westlake's operation and soon plans were drawn up to build a brand new store.

F.K., Ben Barrows, and an unidentified contractor are ready to start building in 1975.

Immediately, the partners began to remodel a larger site across the street to make it viable as a self-service store. The Macon residents were flabbergasted and doubted that it could succeed. "That'll never work," they told Ben. They were wrong. For the next 12 years, the store prospered.

F.K., however, thought that Macon had more potential as a market if the store relocated on the highway east of town. Reluctantly, Ben went to look at a site that F.K. had selected. "It looks like a gully to me," Ben said, but by this

time, everyone knew better than to challenge F.K. Westlake's site selection
ability. The partners built a 12,000 square foot store where the gully used to be.
It did $700,000 worth of business the first year. The downtown store had
done $200,000 worth of business the year before. F.K. knew what he was
talking about.

The Macon location ready for customers

*F.K. (in bow tie) was present at the ribbon-cutting ceremony for the impressive 12,000
square foot Macon store in 1975. The gentleman doing the honors is the mayor of Macon.*

Those Legendary Cookies

Ben Barrows' wife, Lorene, was a woman of many talents. For years, she designed the window displays at the Monroe City store. When Ben moved the store to Macon, Lorene stayed behind to manage the Monroe City operation until the Macon store was ready, and the Monroe City inventory sold down.

What Lorene is most remembered for in company lore, however, are her irresistible Butterscotch Oatmeal Cookies. Long a favorite in the Barrows' household, Lorene began to offer them to the Westlake managers when they made their annual inspection tours. The cookies were such a favorite that the inspectors would dash back for the cookies before they would begin their inspections, better disposed, the Barrows reckoned, to judge the store favorably.

No one was fonder of the cookies than F.K. himself. As he wound down his Westlake career, he would often stop by the Barrows' store to pass the time constructively and to chow down on those cookies. Always prepared, Lorene kept a pre-mixed batch in the refrigerator to be baked should F.K. show up.

Here, for the first time in print, is the cookie recipe that played such an important role in Westlake history.

BUTTERSCOTCH OATMEAL COOKIES

3 cups flour
1½ teaspoons soda
1 teaspoon salt
1½ cups margarine
1½ cups sugar

1½ cups brown sugar
3 eggs, unbeaten
3 cups of quick oats
1½ cups chopped nuts
1½ cups butterscotch bits

Combine flour, baking soda and salt in small bowl. Beat margarine, sugar, brown sugar and vanilla in larger mixer bowl. Add eggs, beating well after each one; then stir in flour mixture and oats. Stir in nuts and butterscotch bits. Chill dough at least one hour. Shape into balls with a teaspoon. Bake on an ungreased cookie sheet 9-12 minutes at 375 degrees. Makes about four dozen scrumptious cookies.

Kirksville joins the family

In 1962, Wade Coorts (left) is congratulated by F.K. as he is made manager-partner of the downtown Kirksville, Missouri, store shown above.

In 1963, F.K. Westlake spied still another north central Missouri city that he wanted to conquer—Kirksville. And this time, he knew just the man he wanted to run it: Wade Coorts, the assistant manager at Jefferson City. Wade accepted the challenge and now, as the fourth of the founding manager-partners, launched the store. In 1972, he and F.K. opened a larger store and expanded it twice again before Wade retired from active management in 1995.

Wade Coorts recalls how the local Chamber of Commerce asked him to close his new Kirksville store at 5 p.m. because that's when the competition closed. Wade told the Chamber that his job was to meet the needs of his customers—not the competition—and he planned to stay open until 9 p.m. Next question?

There was an essential logic to the location of Westlake stores in the 1950s and 1960s. As Al Hall remembers, "Frank wanted to keep all stores within a distance where he could have lunch with a manager and return home for dinner with his wife." F.K. Westlake valued the time with his own family and worked under the assumption that his partners did, too.

Wade Coorts

Bigger and better

Kirksville proved to be such a successful location that it received a larger Westlake's store in the 1970s…then expanded it twice.

Ben Barrows, Paul Kuckelman, Wade Coorts, and Al Hall—sometimes known as "The Big Four" or "The Fab Four" are Westlake legends. At the turn of the 21st century, all four of the men remained active as board members of Westlake Hardware. At that juncture, Ben Barrows had been with the company 54 years, Wade Coorts 41 years, Paul Kuckelman 41 years, and newcomer Al Hall, 39 years. "We just seemed like family," Al Hall remembers. "Every one of us felt like family members."

What made the relationship work was the mutual respect among them and the trusting relationship each man had with F.K. Westlake. "Frank was a very outstanding person," Wade Coorts remembers. "He was very easy to sit down with and talk to about anything and he made me feel good whenever we left the meeting."

"Frank was a very compassionate man," Al Hall adds. "He wasn't a pusher. He let me do what I wanted to do."

"Frank never missed a chance to pat you on the back," notes Ben Barrows. "I think that's important. I think you need that."

Together with F.K., this second generation of shareholders confirmed W.I.'s commitment to customer service and made it the cornerstone of the company as it moved forward. Importantly, in a highly competitive marketplace, they also made this commitment a viable commercial strategy.

"What stays the same in this company," said Paul Kuckelman in his final interview in 2001, "is customer service and personal attention to customer needs. It is one of the things that makes us distinctive and gives us huge advantage over our competition."

"We wanted to be the best neighborhood hardware store in those days," observes Al Hall, cutting to the chase, "and we still want to be the best."

"The life of a hardware clerk is helping customers," says Ben Barrows. "It's a rewarding experience to be able to do that." Helping customers help themselves, in fact, is what Westlake has always been about.

Al Hall tells the story of one of his good customers in Jefferson City, who, with Al's advice, set out to follow his dreams by building his own customized camper off a Winnebago chassis. About a year after he started the project, he drove it down to the hardware store beaming with pride. "This is what I've been doing for the last year," he told Al. "About 80 percent of this came from the Westlake Hardware store."

"It was a nearly perfect thing," Al remembers. "Nearly perfect."

"I built it myself."

Since its inception, Westlake has supplied customers with the tools and goods they've needed to get the job done.

Evening hours

Now busy Americans could shop at their convenience

Number of items sold

Aisle location of item

Additional notations

6,000 candy bars were available, but the supply ran out Thursday at 6:30

Great buys…while they last!

Full page or full spread newspaper advertisements featuring sale items are critical to the retail trade. The Fulton, Missouri, manager added these notations to his copy of the Grand Opening ad which ran May 14, 1968 in the Sun-Gazette.

The Third Generation

RX CONTINUITY

...am _____
...sor WESTLAKE ACE HARDWARE
...arts 3/24/72 Ends tn

MUST BE REHEARSED BEFORE AIRED!

...t's a "Lumberteria"...just one of the new additions
at the new Westlake Ace Hardware...including items like
...cut lumber..molding..paneling..Masonite...and
...........inning..get a load of these specials;
...........hey Easter eggs, 54¢ a bag..
...........pound bag of

Westlake's wins the "Oscar of Retailing"

*F.K. Westlake (left) received the award from
Edward Stehle (right), chairman of the board of
Brand Names Foundation on May 10, 1972.*

The Third Generation

O n May 10, 1972, F.K. Westlake was on top of the world. He had just heard his name announced by no less a personality than Chet Huntley. The fact that he knew he had won in advance did not diminish the thrill. Huntley was among the best-known broadcasters in the world. This was a black-tie event at the Waldorf Astoria in New York. And Westlake Hardware had just been named "National Retailer of the Year."

Specifically, the award commended Westlake for "outstanding retail citizenship, consumer information, and brand name merchandising programs in 1972." For a small town hardware guy from mid-Missouri, honors didn't get much higher than this—the "Oscar of Retailing."

F.K. was particularly pleased to share the honor that glorious night with his son, Scott, then a junior at the University of Missouri. Scott would join the

National honor ceremony is a family affair

Scott Westlake (left) looks on as television anchorman Chet Huntley (center) congratulates F.K. on receiving this prestigious award.

Howard Elsberry

company full time when he graduated. Nor was Scott the only third generation member of the extended Westlake family enthused by the family business.

Some years earlier, F.K. Westlake had convinced his son-in-law Howard Elsberry that his future was in the hardware industry. After graduating from college with a degree in business administration, Howard Elsberry had taken a managerial post with TG&Y, then a respected retail chain. A firm believer in entrepreneurship, F.K. persuaded Howard that as good a future he might have at TG&Y, he was never going to own a part of it. F.K. proved highly persuasive. "You didn't work for Frank," Howard remembers. "You worked with him."

Howard launched his Westlake career in Columbia under the guidance of Paul Kuckelman. In 1967, F.K. offered Howard partnership in a Westlake Hardware in Fulton, Missouri, a town best known as the site of Winston Churchill's "Iron Curtain" speech just 20 years earlier.

On May 15, 1968, Fulton Mayor W.C. Murphy cut the ribbon on a new Westlake's Ace Hardware, whose 16,200 square feet were stocked with 25,000 items. Among the advertised items were household brooms on sale for 87¢, bathroom tissue 5¢ a roll, laundry baskets for 44¢, and Lucite wall paint at $4.97 a gallon (regularly $6.39).

Fulton comes aboard

Howard managed the Westlake's store in Fulton, built in 1968. This is a later photograph, ca. 1982.

When last mentioned to the reader, young Doug Burton was hammering nails into the floor of his grandfather's store in Huntsville. W.I. served as Doug's surrogate father until his widowed mom, Martha Will remarried. After their marriage, Nathan Casto and Martha Will bought a hardware store in Brunswick, Missouri. Doug worked there throughout his teens, delivering Uregas, selling appliances, and vowing that the last thing he would do as an adult is work in a hardware store.

While studying for a Master's in Finance at the University of Missouri, however, Doug needed a way to support himself and went to work for Paul Kuckelman in Columbia. Much to his own surprise, Doug discovered he loved the business. He left school and took a job as assistant manager at the new Westlake Hardware in Mexico, Missouri.

Another "family-run" store

In 1970, Doug Burton became assistant manager of the Mexico, Missouri, store shown above.

Hardware and more

A spacious interior with a wide range of goods greeted the customer upon entering the Mexico, Missouri, store.

In 1971, F.K. Westlake partnered with his nephew Doug Burton to launch a new venture in Chillicothe, Missouri. The new 18,000 square foot store opened with a flourish in Chillicothe's Southtown Shopping Center on October 18, 1971. The sale price of tissue rolls had jumped from 5¢ to 6¢ since the Fulton opening three years earlier, but otherwise it was just as attractive a sale.

A different path...
to the same destination

In 1972, the same year that F.K. was honored with the
retailing Oscar, his daughter Anne Elsberry took a major step that
one day would lead her back to the family business as well.

With the youngest of her three children now in kindergarten,
she headed off to law school at the University of Missouri, to which
she commuted from her Fulton home. Not unlike her grandmother
Scottie, Anne was ambitious and adventurous and not afraid to
chart an unorthodox course. She would practice law for 19 years—
first in Moberly and then in Kansas City. In 1994, she would leave
private practice and join Westlake as senior vice president and
general counsel. She is now actively involved in the real estate,
human resources, and risk management areas, as well as the role
of chief legal officer for the company.

Anne Westlake Elsberry

*This photo was taken when Anne
was working for Kansas City law
firm Lathrop and Gage.*

Taking stock

In May 1973, F.K. Westlake was a partner in the nine stores that made up the Westlake family, all separate corporations. The locations and the partners are listed below:

Moberly:	**wholly owned by F.K. Westlake**
Columbia East:	**Kenny Dickson, Paul Kuckelman**
Jefferson City:	**Kenny Dickson, Paul Kuckelman, Al Hall**
Macon:	**Ben Barrows**
Kirksville:	**Wade Coorts**
Columbia West:	**Kenny Dickson, Paul Kuckelman**
Fulton:	**Howard Elsberry**
Mexico:	**Kenny Dickson**
Chillicothe:	**Doug Burton**

Although the Mexico store had been expanded to 20,000 square feet in 1970, the Kirksville store to 25,000 square feet in 1972, and the Moberly store to 25,000 square feet in 1973, the Columbia East store remained the largest in the family at 32,000 square feet. (In just four years, the Columbia West store would move to a 48,000 square foot location. It is still the largest store in the Westlake family.)

The central office and warehouse remained in Moberly, but the decision-making in the company was largely decentralized. Managers were responsible for hiring and firing, selecting their own product line, running their own promotions, and ordering their own merchandise. "Excessive internal control kills a store," said F.K. Westlake, "and causes it to lose individuality."

The stores at the time were altogether rich in individuality. F.K. divided them into two divisions—north of Moberly and south of Moberly. F.K. did this

THOSE WESTLAKES of MISSOURI

A TIME FOR MOVING AHEAD

While many others are standing still because of the economic situation, Westlake's Ace Hardware chain of Moberly is forging ahead, establishing new outlets and expanding existing ones. Here is the story of Westlake's, its philosophy of business and a glimpse into the dynamism of the organization.

Chances are a good many of the folks in central Missouri have, at one time or another, heard of Westlake's Ace Hardware. And, chances are equally good that they live within a trading area of a Westlake store and they've seen the popular TV show "Wally's Workshop," sponsored by Westlake's.

This young and progressive chain of hardware stores, based in Moberly, is growing at the rate of a store per year. There are nine outlets. A 10th one is scheduled for opening later this year. They are located in Columbia (two), Chillicothe, Fulton, Jefferson City, Kirksville, Macon and Mexico. The 10th Westlake's will go up in Blue Springs, outside of Kansas City, Mo. The time is not far off when this chain will expand out of the central region and will blanket the entire state. Add to all this a 1,000-acre working farm, and you get a good idea of the scope of this remarkable organization.

And all this, in spite of a sluggish economy and the prophets of doom who advise a laying-low policy until things blow over. The Westlake people will have none of this. They want to forge ahead, because it is their belief that economical situation or not, now is the time for expansion. Existing stores and land may be had at bargain prices.

The guiding hands at the helm of Westlake's are Frank W. Westlake, president; Howard Elsberry, vice president of operations; and Scott Westlake, who will manage the Blue Springs store and who has had an active hand in the expansion of the chain. Dynamism is the keynote with the Westlake Group.

It has always been so, since the early humble beginnings with a small hardware store in Huntsville, Mo., in 1903, owned by Frank's father. Young Frank cut his teeth on hardware at that store for the munificent sum of $100 per year. He worked after school and weekends. The hardware bug bit him hard during those early years, and he desparately wanted to own his own store.

Corporate officers of Westlake Hardware pose at firm's Moberly headquarters. From left to right: Howard Elsberry, vice president of operations; Frank Westlake, president; and Scott Westlake, presidential assistant and future manager of the Blue Springs outlet.

A view of the 25,000 sq. ft. Westlake Hardware Co. of Moberly, Inc., Moberly, Mo., which houses the corporate offices of Westlake Hardware Co. The design and identification of this store is standard for the firm's other eight outlets.

An early photograph showing the first Westlake store in Huntsville, Mo., around 1903, owned by Frank Westlake's father. Young Frank accumulated his first experience in the hardware business in this store, before striking out on his own and founding the present chain of outlets. Notice the wood stoves at right, and the horsecollars above them.

An expanding enterprise

Not including Blue Springs, (added in 1975), this graphic shows a good representation of the Missouri Westlake locations in the early 1970s. Westlake's Ace Hardware was featured in the April 1975 edition of Hardware Merchandiser.

both to build camaraderie and stoke competition. If the north stores generated the greatest sales increase in a given year, the south managers would treat the winning managers to dinner and vice versa. After a particularly good year, Howard Elsberry remembers Wade Coorts being rewarded with two 16-ounce steaks that he downed at one sitting. Even now, running a hardware store is a physically demanding job. At that time, it was even more rigorous.

To be sure, this was a different era. "Everything back then was manual," says one veteran manager, "and labor intensive." In an era before forklifts, a truckload of, say, peat moss would be unloaded a bag at a time. In an era before perpetual inventory systems, managers would wheel a large catalogue through the aisles on a cart and check the status of every item. In an era before bar codes and electronic scanners, managers would note the price of each item with a black marker.

Pre-scanning days

Before the electronic age, pricing goods took time and energy. Each item needed to be individually stamped or tagged.

Trade magazine articles from the period speak of the Westlake stores' cleanliness and modernity but inevitably comment on a certain shared "flavor" highly suggestive of "an old fashioned general store."

With as many as 25,000 different products to choose among, managers made some highly distinctive choices. Some of the stores had Hallmark Card shops in their housewares departments as a way to stimulate traffic and to reinforce the self-service image of the store. In the Columbia stores, Paul Kuckelman stocked over-the-counter drugs at discount prices, again to encourage traffic. Some of the larger stores had designated "Craft Shops" partly in the belief that they attracted college students and other younger customers.

"A breadth of goods brings business," observed F.K. Westlake. A consumer survey from the time confirmed his intuition. It listed "variety, selection, and stock depth" as the number one reason

A reflection of individual tastes and ideas

Each Westlake's Ace Hardware store reflected the business philosophy of its manager. The Kirksville store chose to include a Hallmark Card shop and a "Bride's Corner" with all types of suitable wedding gifts.

customers chose to shop at Westlake. "Courteous, friendly, helpful employees" came in a close second.

These friendly, helpful managers inevitably took an interest in their communities. They sponsored Little League baseball teams, softball leagues, the United Way, the Boy Scouts, their churches, the local and state Chamber, a wide variety of schools and colleges, and even law enforcement programs like "Operation Identification." Community involvement has always been a useful way to raise a store's profile. But F.K. Westlake made a point of hiring the kind of people who like to help out in the community, whether it helped the business or not.

Community ties

The Westlake store in Jefferson City chose to sponsor this Nine-Year-Old Midget League baseball team in the 1970s.

Selling one's wares

A variety of good spirited promotions reinforced the general store feel of the Westlake enterprise in the early 1970s. A series of Handy Hints advertorials featured the likes of "Uncle Doug" Burton, "Uncle Wade" Coorts, and "Cuzzin Howard" Elsberry sharing some useful bits of hardware knowledge with the community.

A related advertorial featured a Handy Hint Contest in which customers were encouraged to submit their own useful advice. One typical ad of the period congratulated Mrs. Jess Dowlin of Mexico, Missouri, for her excellent idea on how to preserve putty. "Put it in a plastic bag to keep it moist," she suggested. "Knead the putty inside the bag to a working consistency." For her ingenuity, Mrs. Dowlin won $200—a considerable sum at that time.

In a particularly ambitious promotion, one of the Columbia stores sent a staff manager out in to the community to give away the top of a sugar bowl. Inside the top was the message that if the lucky recipient came to Westlake Hardware, he or she could retrieve the bottom half of the sugar bowl free. The promotion generated "a good deal of traffic." Although the store was left with a fair share of unmatched bottoms, these could still be sold as separate items—unlike, say, unmatched tops.

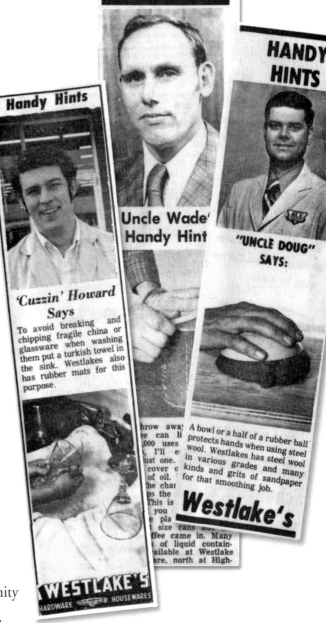

Advice from family members

The Westlake "relatives" had weekly advice to impart to customers that helped solve or alleviate household dilemmas.

Time out for fun

Wade Coorts and Al Hall (in center), with associates from their stores, boarded a bus one Sunday morning and took a trip to a St. Louis Cardinals baseball game. At that time, Missouri's "blue laws" prevailed and retail stores did not open for business on Sundays.

Other promotions were geared to attract children. The Fulton store sponsored a pumpkin-carving contest. The Moberly store promoted a two-day "Goat Alley" for the kids. "Come pet the goats," read the flyer. "Feed them, too."

By the early 1970s, however, stores were trending away from gimmicks and towards hardware fundamentals like plumbing and electrical. In a highly useful promotion, some stores offered free seminars in electrical and plumbing basics.

Although they retained their individuality, the stores also were beginning to work together. The first company-wide newspaper circular ran in 1969. While the individual stores handled their own regular, weekly advertising until the 1980s, they now began coordinating a few company-wide circulars each year.

In the 1970s, Westlake Hardware started experimenting with television. One series of TV ads featured "famous radio and television personality Dennis James." James held the distinction of announcing the first-ever television advertisement before going on to host game shows *Name That Tune* and *The Price is Right*. In key mid-Missouri markets, Westlake Hardware also sponsored a syndicated weekly show called *Wally's Workshop*.

Central exchange

It was the central office too that managed the Ace shipments, 80 percent of the stores' total merchandise. Once or twice a week, truckers from the Ace distribution center in Lincoln, Nebraska, would hook up with their counterparts from Westlake and swap trailers at a convenient truck stop in Rockport, Missouri. The Westlake trucks would distribute goods to the various stores on their way back to Moberly.

In addition to this function, the central office was responsible for sending out monthly profit and loss statements and taking care of government forms. As to computers, the company did use one for accounting. A 1974 trade magazine reporter, however, took quaintly ironic comfort in the fact that, "The electronic monster has not taken over yet."

Electronic monsters

In the "old days," computers were massive units kept in separate rooms. Workstations were developed that would feed into the mainframe. Portable, personal computers would not reach widespread public awareness until the early 1980s.

Westlake's "HQ"

(Top) Modest by today's standards, the central office of Westlake Hardware was housed in the former Woodland Hospital building in Moberly from 1982 to 1990.

(Right) F.K. Westlake behind the desk in his Moberly office.

The company was on the cusp of a new age in the mid-1970s, not just technologically, but managerially. In 1975, F.K. brought Howard Elsberry to the central office in Moberly as Vice President of Operations to help plan where and how expansions and other store innovations would take place.

Among those innovations was a separate corporation that Howard initiated called Dealer's Wholesale, Inc., or DWI—an acronym that even then looked a wee bit peculiar when seen on a truck. By setting up a separate entity, however, the company was able to negotiate wholesale prices from a wide range of major vendors. For several years, in fact, DWI served as a wholesaler for companies other than Westlake, including Wal-Mart. Howard's experience with just about every function of the business would serve him well when he assumed the company's top job some years later.

Different era, different meaning...
In the mid-1970s "DWI" was a good thing for Westlake's—resulting in lower business costs and better distribution.

"Economy notwithstanding, we are constantly planning for new stores," F.K. Westlake told a reporter from the *Hardware Merchandiser* in April 1975. "We don't want to push any faster than that, because we can only generate so much cash for projects. We prefer to generate our own funds for expansions."

F.K. Westlake was voicing the philosophy that guided the company for its first seventy years and that guides it today. The philosophy has proved a productive and viable one. It is the rare enterprise that prospers for 100 years, let alone under continuous management. That Westlake Hardware has done both is a testament to the rock solid foundation on which it was built.

Bringing a personal touch to management

F.K. Westlake inspects merchandise in the Columbia store, ca. 1975. Although many new stores were being added at this time, the emphasis remained on quality goods and economic stability.

F.K. was "constantly planning for new stores"

From St. Joseph, Missouri (top) to Shawnee, Kansas (left), to Omaha, Nebraska (bottom) F.K. believed that when the time was right (and the money was there), another store would be added to the ever-growing Westlake network.

Suburban expansion

Tom Terrell

In 1974, Scott Westlake graduated from the University of Missouri and joined the company. Just one year later, F.K. chose Scott to manage the company's most adventurous enterprise since self-service. Westlake Hardware was opening its first store in a major market, Blue Springs, Missouri—a fast-growing Kansas City suburb.

Bill Dickson traces Westlake's interest in Kansas City back to 1969, when the company was looking for a tenant for the Mexico shopping center. Most of the potential tenants were headquartered in the Kansas City area and Bill remembers repeated trips and visits to area hardware stores.

In 1975, Kansas City was the talk of the nation. In the last three years alone it had opened a new international airport, the nation's most ambitious private urban development called Crown Center, a new basketball arena, and two state-of-the-art ballparks in one complex. Better still, the baseball team, the Kansas City Royals, was on the verge of launching a mini-dynasty that would net the team at least a half-dozen division championships and a World Series victory in the next ten years. At least half of the players lived in Blue Springs. That was the place to be, and Westlake Hardware was there too. The store succeeded nicely, and a year later, the company was prepared to open a second Kansas City store.

Tom Terrell remembers that second store well. Just a few years out of high school, he had started with Westlake in Fulton in 1973 under Howard Elsberry. Tom learned quickly and in February 1976 was offered the job as assistant manager at the new Kansas City store located in the city's north suburbs. Today, Tom Terrell is Westlake's senior vice president and chief operating officer.

Big-city expansion

The Blue Springs location (center) was strategically placed in suburban Kansas City. The Westlake store was just a few miles east of the stadium complex and minutes away from downtown Kansas City.

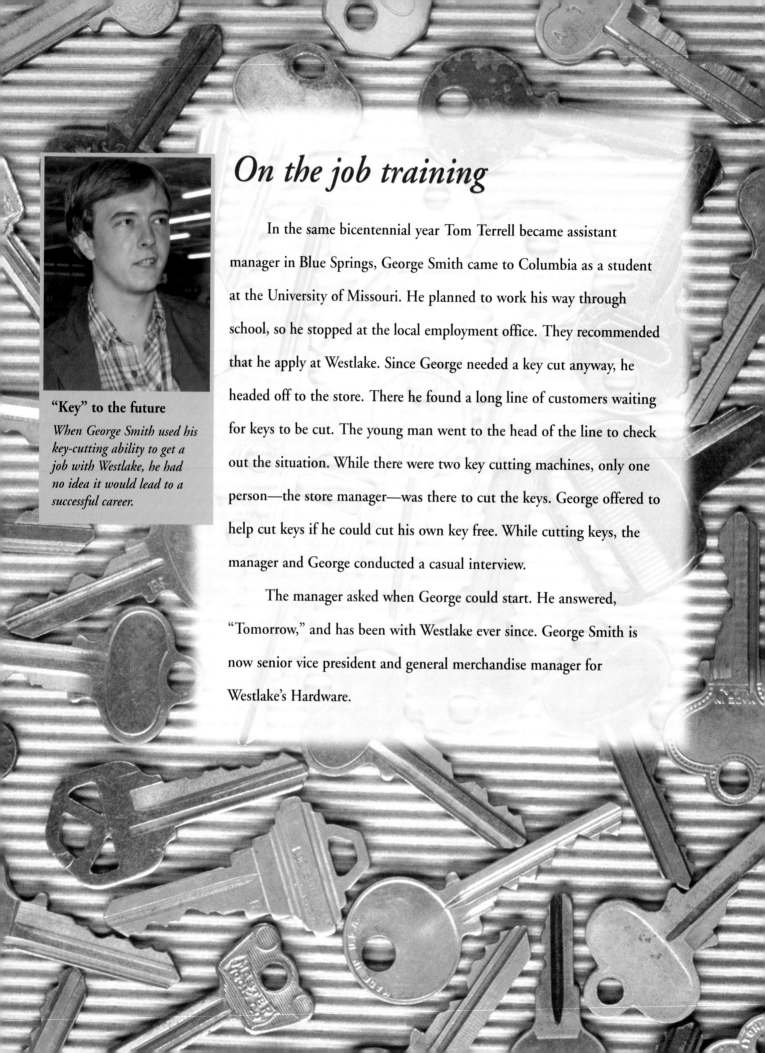

On the job training

In the same bicentennial year Tom Terrell became assistant manager in Blue Springs, George Smith came to Columbia as a student at the University of Missouri. He planned to work his way through school, so he stopped at the local employment office. They recommended that he apply at Westlake. Since George needed a key cut anyway, he headed off to the store. There he found a long line of customers waiting for keys to be cut. The young man went to the head of the line to check out the situation. While there were two key cutting machines, only one person—the store manager—was there to cut the keys. George offered to help cut keys if he could cut his own key free. While cutting keys, the manager and George conducted a casual interview.

The manager asked when George could start. He answered, "Tomorrow," and has been with Westlake ever since. George Smith is now senior vice president and general merchandise manager for Westlake's Hardware.

"Key" to the future

When George Smith used his key-cutting ability to get a job with Westlake, he had no idea it would lead to a successful career.

Going to Kansas City

F.K. Westlake, nearing 70 and still active in the company, gave his last substantive on-camera interview in 1984. He spoke with great pride about the company's past and even greater anticipation about the company's future.

The store count in 1984 stood at 28. In 1983, for the first time in its history, Westlake Hardware had opened multiple new stores in a given market, with two stores in Oklahoma City and three in Omaha. In that same year, the company opened a regional office in the Kansas City suburb of Overland Park, Kansas. Those who saw this move as a harbinger of things to come would soon be proved right.

Overcoming losses...and rebuilding

As Westlake's stores were springing up all over the Midwest, two stores came down... unexpectedly. On September 21, 1977, just after its Grand Opening, the Olathe store #13 (yes, number 13), caught fire. According to newpaper accounts, the fire "totally destroyed the contents of the building and burned a hole in the roof." Construction began immediately on the new store, which re-opened in the spring of 1978 (shown above). It took quite a few years before Westlake's decided to use the number 13 again!

As bad as the picture above looks, the Fulton store did not burn down completely on Sunday, October 25, 1998. The Fulton fire department literally stood with their backs pressed to the turpentine and paint thinner displays to fight the fire. The store opened again just four days later on Thursday, October 29. Eventually the store was completely remodeled in 1999. At left, Fulton residents line up in anticipation for the Grand Opening of the Westlake's Hallmark store adjacent to the hardware store.

1984 marked the end of an era as well. F.K.'s sister, Martha Will, and her husband retired from their small hardware business in Brunswick, Missouri. Their retirement marked the end of the early, rural Westlake stores. The Shelbina and Huntsville stores had been sold to their respective managers; Monroe City had moved to Macon. "You won't find any of the stores before self-service," boasted F.K. with scarcely a trace of nostalgia. None had to be closed. All had phased themselves out gracefully or had been sold to their managers. And F.K. was clearly looking to the future.

Scott Westlake

As F.K. knew, however, that future was not to be his to shape. F.K. began to phase himself out gracefully as well and confidently turned the business over to the next generation, initially to son Scott who emerged as just the third head of Westlake Hardware in its 80-year history. With F.K.'s blessing, Scott introduced two significant and potentially useful changes in the way the company was run. Both took place in 1986, the year the World Series championship flag flew over Royals stadium.

The first involved corporate structure. The company consolidated the mini-corporations that F.K. had set up—now an awkward 13—into one. This roll-up ceremoniously went into effect on January 1, 1987. The partners in the

A merge of partners

Ben Barrows, Paul Kuckelman, Wade Coorts, and Al Hall consolidated their operations in 1986 and became shareholders in one new corporation.

A westward shift

Westlake's corporate headquarters at 15501 W. 99th Street in Lenexa, Kansas, gave the company a more centralized location, and moved it much closer to transportation hubs.

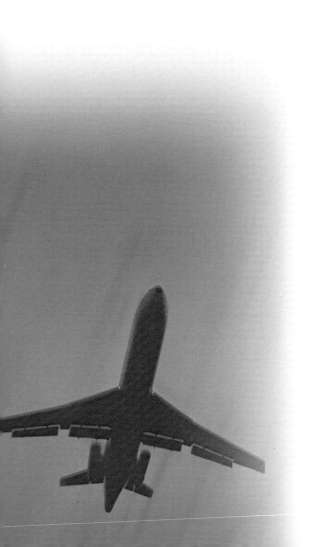

separate stores emerged as shareholders in the larger corporation. These included Ben Barrows, Paul Kuckelman, Wade Coorts, and Al Hall, the "Big Four," as Tom Terrell remembers them.

Just as dramatically, the company moved its headquarters from Moberly to the Kansas City suburb of Lenexa, Kansas. This move made a good deal of sense. The Westlake geography had shifted from the heart of Missouri to the heart of America. Kansas City was as central to the latter as Moberly was to the former, and Kansas City was much easier to access by truck and rail, and especially by plane.

Expanding horizons

Anything seemed possible in the 1980s, not just for Westlake, but for the country as a whole. In particular, the do-it-yourself industry was booming—even though "hardware store" wasn't the preferred label. The new and improved label was "home center" and serious debates were held over just what store qualified for that title. It seemed as if every company was growing, adding stores, or merging to create an even bigger company. Westlake was no exception. The company had begun in 1980 with 14 stores. At the end of 1988, there were 48 Westlake stores in the Midwest Division.

Important changes had been made in this decade. The Westlake organization had started as a loose-knit confederation or "family" of individual stores. By the end of the 1980s, a single corporate structure was taking shape.

Making the headlines

Westlake's continued to make national hardware news—even being featured as the cover story of the June 1988 Home Center *magazine. This photo features the store interior in Lenexa, Kansas.*

MAJOR LEAGUE FORMULA

Just another hardware store? Better think twice. Westlake Hardware could become the first national chain of its kind.

By Holly Jenks/Feature Editor and Mark L. Johnson/Associate Editor

Hardware stores compete in a league sometimes thought of as the minors. But one hardware chain's growth ranks it among the majors: Westlake Hardware Inc., Lenexa, Kan.

Westlake Hardware, its franchised Lone Star Hardware Inc., San Antonio, Texas, and its acquisition-minded president, Scott Westlake, run All-Star caliber stores. Not once in 75 years has a Westlake store been closed.

"Scott's got a very successful formula. I didn't recognize it existed. Then I met Scott, and I started to understand," said Tom Seifert, president of 22 franchised stores in Florida. "It's probably one of the best formulas in the business."

Power hardware

Call the Westlake formula a "power hardware store." The idea is to fill markets with 30,000-square-foot stores stocking a big selection of hardware items.

"When you say 'hardware store,' a lot of people get in their head a 6,000-square-footer. Ours are bigger," said Daryl Lansdale, president of seven franchised stores in Texas. "We're a specialty retailer. Our business is selection."

There was a time when Westlake Hardware was just a "hardware store," the less-than-6,000-square-foot variety. Seventy-five years ago Scott Westlake's grandfather opened a small store in rural Missouri. Today, the company packs merchandise into stores averaging 13 times the original's size. But the allure of Westlake Hardware, and its family of franchises, is not the individual size of each store, but the number of them: 77 today, growing 20 percent in number each year.

"Scott Westlake definitely has his sights on something that I would call a national chain," Seifert said.

While not actively seeking acquisitions at the moment, Scott Westlake did suggest he isn't finished stalking possibilities.

"We need some time to digest the businesses we just acquired," he said.

To understand Westlake Hardware, think of Scott Westlake as principal owner of two baseball teams: Westlake Hardware and Lone Star Hardware. The teams play in the same league but in separate stadiums, each managed autonomously.

The first team, Westlake Hardware Inc. (WHI), has three divisions: Westlake Midwest ($105 million in projected 1988 sales); the Direct Mail & Catalog Division (see page 55); and the WHI division, the firm's accounting and real estate arm.

WHI was incorporated on Dec. 31, 1986. Prior to that date, Westlake was an amalgamation of 13 separate companies. Basically, the Westlake family, a few partners and original store managers all had ownership stakes. The new corporation consolidated their interests and formed divisions to keep decision-making far down the chain of command.

Team Two is Lone Star Hardware Inc., operating 29 stores in Texas, New Mexico and Florida. Lone Star is comprised of two divisions, both franchising the Westlake name. The Southwest Division, headed by Daryl Lansdale (formerly president and CEO of W.R. Grace's Central Division), currently operates seven stores. The Florida Division is made up of 22 units. Twenty-one were former Lindsley Home Centers, plus one new unit opened in February. The Florida Division is headed by Tom Seifert.

But why structure Lone Star separately and franchise the Westlake name?

"We wanted Lone Star to be a growth vehicle," Westlake said. "Lone Star was set up with the idea that we wouldn't make my father and his generation stockholders in the new Lone Star company. Basically, the ownership of Lone Star would be a younger group of people."

Westlake Hardware received much attention when it announced the formation of Lone Star Hardware in April 1987, and again in October 1987 when the Lindsley stores were acquired from a holding company representing Evans Products Co. In actuality, the Westlake chain had been growing by chunks of four to eight stores per year since 1983.

"I don't think we've ever put any outside limits on our growth," Westlake said. "We want to grow as fast as we can as long as we can pick up all the pieces."

Inside Westlake's Lenexa, Kan., store: Back walls are visible from the entrance, and new colorful signs quickly capture attention.

52/HOME CENTER Magazine/JUNE 1988

Howard Elsberry

Howard became Westlake's CEO in 1991 and serves in that role as the company begins its second 100 years.

Advertising and promotional merchandising had been consolidated—with the store manager still controlling regular merchandise. Market districts were created and district managers were named. Cindy Mason, now vice president, established Westlake's first human resources department.

Westlake had begun the decade as a well-respected, nationally known company. By the late 1980s, anything Westlake did was news in the industry. When Westlake established a franchise operation called "Lone Star," with stores in the Texas/New Mexico area and in Florida, that was also big news.

Like many other companies of the time, though, Westlake's rapid expansion came to an equally sudden pause as the company digested what it had swallowed.

Upon Scott Westlake's resignation to pursue other interests, Westlake established an Executive Committee to govern the company and search for a new CEO. The committee found Richard Mitchell, formerly with Zales Jewellers, and tapped him for the position of CEO.

Under Richard Mitchell's guidance, Westlake closed the Florida operation, pulled the promising Texas/New Mexico stores into the Westlake organization, and closed the unprofitable stores. Lone Star ceased to exist. Richard Mitchell also proved resourceful in getting the company's debt restructured and setting up the systems and business practices that Westlake needed.

From the beginning of Richard's employment, it was understood that this was a transitional time. Richard was nearing retirement age when he took the position with Westlake. In two years, after he had set Westlake on a new business footing and groomed his successor, Richard retired to his native Georgia.

Howard Elsberry assumed Westlake's top job on April 1, 1991. Soon after, the company opened its first new store in three years. While Westlake still intended to grow, there was more emphasis now on "controlled growth."

On January 22, 1992, an era came to an end. After several years of failing health, F.K. Westlake died at the age of 76. He had lived a productive and noble life. The obituary told of how he was survived by his wife, Virginia, and his three loving children (Anne, Scott and Richard), how he had volunteered with the Boy Scouts, the Trinity Union Methodist Church, the Moberly Area Chamber of Commerce, and the Missouri State Chamber, and how he had once won the "Oscar of Retailing."

His goal, continued the obituary, "was to have the best hardware stores in the country." That he had accomplished his goal, no one could deny.

F.K. Westlake

With his visionary insight, practical know-how and uncommon common sense, F.K. Westlake had served his company well for more than 50 years.

"Mr. Frank K. Westlake has been a source of inspiration for not only youth, but hundreds of adults as well. He demonstrates, through example, that service to others is not only a responsibility, but a privilege, of our great free enterprise system of American business."

From a recommendation letter written by the Scout Executive of the Columbia chapter of the Boy Scouts of America, dated December 4, 1972

Westlake family traditions

Westlake team members include the younger generations, too, as children and grandchildren follow in their parents' and grandparents' footsteps.

(Left top) Howard Elsberry, his son Steve Elsberry and grandson Andrew enjoy a perfect day at Kauffman Stadium. Westlake sponsored the Kansas City Symphony's performance with fireworks that followed a Royals game. Howard threw out the first pitch for the game.

(Right top) Brian Kuckelman, his sister Susan Leonard and her son Ted attend the Grand Opening of store #76 in Hays, Kansas.

Back to the future?

Doug Burton shows his grandson Burton how to handle a hammer. Unlike Doug, little Burton won't be driving nails in the floor of his grandfather's store to help pass the time. But perhaps he will carry on the family tradition of "helping America help itself."

94

The Future

Board of Directors

Back row: Bill Dickson, Al Hall, Leo Carney, Richard Westlake, Doug Burton, Doug Cleaveland, Wade Coorts
Front row: Scott Westlake, Steve Elsberry, Anne Elsberry, Ben Barrows, Jane Kuckelman, Howard Elsberry, Susan Leonard

Officers of Westlake

Back row: Jim Crumpler (Senior Vice President/CFO), Tom Terrell (Senior Vice President/COO), Doug Burton (Executive Vice President – Marketing and Development), Tom Leir (Vice President – Information Services)

Front row: George Smith (Senior Vice President, General Merchandise Manager), Cindy Mason (Vice President – Human Resources), Anne Elsberry (Senior Vice President/General Counsel), Howard Elsberry (President/CEO)

The Future

When Columbia East opened in 1965, it was the largest hardware store around. Soon after, "home centers" such as Handy Dan and Central Hardware came on the scene with stores at least twice the size of Columbia. The next generation of big stores began on June 22, 1979, when Bernie Marcus and Arthur Blank opened the first Home Depot store in Atlanta, Georgia. Since then, "big box" or "warehouse" stores have opened in virtually every large market and many medium to small markets across the company. Without a doubt, these "big boxes" present a serious challenge for smaller hardware stores and other retailers.

Westlake Hardware had the good fortune to redefine itself just before the big-box era began in earnest. The redefinition was simple enough. "We got back to our roots," says CEO Howard Elsberry. The fact is, Westlake Hardware had been dealing with competition since the first day W.I. Westlake bought into the Huntsville store. If it wasn't the "Hardware Man" of Huntsville, it was the "Hardware Men" of Moberly, or more threatening still, the mail order catalogue houses that threatened to suck the life out of small town commerce. None of them deterred Westlake Hardware, nor would the warehouse stores.

As the company moved into the 21st century, Westlake continued to prosper because management understood its mission. That mission was to be America's best neighborhood hardware store. "Best" now implied not only high levels of convenience and service, but also of sophistication. The company set out to prove that new technology, well applied, could make an enterprise more human—not less.

Columbia past and present—as different as night and day?

The Columbia Westlake's Ace Hardware store in 1965 (top) and its surroundings may look quite different from its counterpart today (bottom). Today's Westlake stores offer a vast assortment of goods from all over the world that the early manager/partners could only dream of, but one thing remains constant—the integrity of the Westlake name and what it stands for.

In an era when the competition was becoming increasingly faceless, and its service increasingly more remote, Westlake's emphasis on humanity would come to define the company into the future.

To assure that the service Westlake delivers is of the highest and most consistent quality, Westlake set up a comprehensive corporate training department. At a hardware store, service means more than the ability to smile and say, "Have a nice day." It means knowing what literally thousands of items are designed to do and how any number of in-home systems are meant to work. For a century, Westlake Hardware has been helping America help itself. In the big-box era, this task is becoming more and more uniquely Westlake's.

Emphasis on humanity

Westlake's avoids the "big box" approach of warehouse-type hardware stores. As shown below, the architecture of this Lee's Summit, Missouri, store blends in well with the surrounding neighboorhood, and welcomes customers with a "hometown" look.

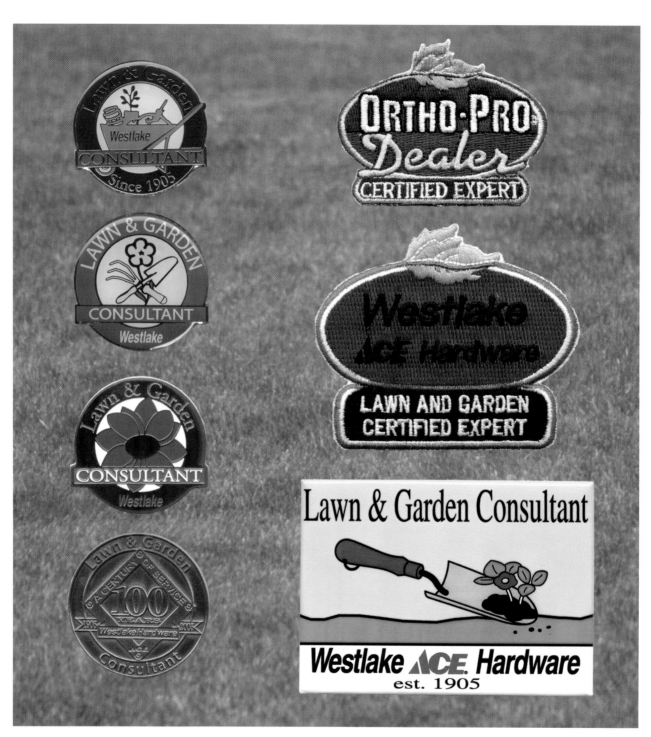

Training green thumbs in the ranks

For several years, Westlake has trained associates in lawn and garden care. After attending a class and passing the exam, associates are deemed Lawn & Garden Consultants, and receive a pin to signify their status. At first, patches and badges were given (right), then pins (left) took their place. The lower left button for 2005 displays the special 100th Anniversary logo.

"At a lot of the box stores, they know where an item is—sometimes," says one veteran store manager, "but they don't know how to fix hardly anything."

Service, of course, is predicated on hiring and retaining good people, and this is a task that Howard Elsberry takes as seriously as F.K. Westlake. "The people still come first," Elsberry observes. They have to. Despite the centralization of some key functions, the managers retain a good deal of autonomy. "We get to run our store practically like we own it," observes one manager.

Typically, when opening a new store, the company will choose someone from within the ranks who has already proved his or her abilities. A sophisticated training program assures that the associates who do move through the ranks are capable and committed to the mission of managing America's best neighborhood hardware stores. The program focuses on creating leaders. These are people who can get work done through inspiring others, thus creating opportunity for the next generation of leaders. To keep good practices alive, the department draws on the experiences of managers from the past—like F.K. Westlake and Paul Kuckelman. Paul, who trained many Westlake managers and executives, would be proud to know that his daughter Jane Kuckelman helps sustain company tradition by leading training sessions in the appropriately named Kuckelman Conference Room.

Leadership takes a front seat

Jane Kuckelman (center) helps train associates in the Kuckelman Conference Room, named after her father Paul Kuckelman.

To improve productivity and to free more associates for a direct service role, Westlake Hardware has implemented several necessary technological refinements. Some years back, the company installed a state-of-the-art Merchandising Management System (MMS) from the JDA Software Group. This system, arguably the world's most popular, provided Westlake with fully integrated merchandising and financial applications for its multiple locations. Its features included purchase order management, a module for warehouse management, as well as reporting tools to track vendors, profit, accounts payable, and other critical financial variables.

The "good old days" of ordering merchandise in the 1980s

If body language says anything, these Westlake associates may have been less than thrilled with this tedious but important part of their job. The wooden portable "desk" was wheeled from aisle to aisle as the department manager checked over the inventory item by item to determine the weekly order.

Taking stock in the 21st century

Scanning and bar coding has streamlined product inventory, shaving hours off of the process. Computerized summaries allow the store manager to quickly evaluate inventory movement within the system and to place orders efficiently.

In the early part of the new century, when the company went looking for a new inventory replenishment system, Westlake executives discovered that JDA had just bought the E3 system they had their eyes on. They then began to implement this system region by region.

For the store managers, it meant a new and liberating way of doing business. Instead of having to review the inventory each week manually and order accordingly, they now watch as the E3 system reviews the inventory automatically. The system then draws up its own orders, tailored to the season and each store's particular needs. Managers retain the responsibility to review the order and accept or modify as they see fit, but virtually all of the detail work has been done for them.

Hitting the highway

Besides their obvious use for transporting goods, these 18-wheelers make perfect moving billboards. As the trucks make regular runs between the warehouse and the stores, fellow motorists can't help but notice the Westlake name and featured product. Like on earlier metal building signs, co-op advertising is often used.

Keeping the shelves stocked

Warehouse storage allows for quick sorting and transporting of goods. Forklifts move pallets of merchandise that is stacked high and deep in the 225,000 square-foot warehouse at 14000 Marshall.

The E3 system also determines whether the order goes to the expanded Westlake warehouse in Lenexa, to any of four Ace retail supply centers, or to another vendor. The system cuts the purchase order as well.

As Westlake Hardware completes its first century, management has completed the implementation of this system company-wide and is now establishing best practices throughout. After a hundred years, the company stock

Westlake's centralized operation in Lenexa, Kansas

*Westlake moved its headquarters and distribution center to this huge facility at 14000
Marshall Drive in 2005.*

remains largely in the hands of the people who built the company and their direct descendants. The "Big Four" are now only three—Ben Barrows, Wade Coorts, and Al Hall—but these gentlemen continue to play an active and critical role, not only in setting the direction of the company, but also in establishing the continuity with the company's past.

"The Board loves the hardware business," observes Howard Elsberry.

Each year, in fact, several board members as well as a representative contingent from the front office make a series of inspection tours throughout the Westlake territory. In the company tradition, they make these tours by bus. The touring inspectors—20 to 25 strong—begin their routes in late September and continue through to early November, making perhaps five separate trips in all and visiting every Westlake store before the inspections are completed.

A strong partnership continues

Westlake's was awarded the President's Cup from Ace Hardware in 1996. From left, Ace CEO Dave Hodnik, Westlake CEO Howard Elsberry, store manager Brian Richards, and Bill Loftus of Ace Hardware. This award recognizes Westlake as the Best Ace Hardware Store in the country.

Making the grade

Al Hall (right) makes a few notes during the Board's annual inspection of Westlake stores. Howard Elsberry (second from left) chats with a store associate for his perspective on the store's operation.

This tradition began more than forty years ago. Back then, the store managers would pile into a couple of Westlake station wagons and hit the road. What made these early tours particularly energizing is that the managers would visit each other's stores. "We cleaned up and got everything shipshape," Ben Barrows remembers fondly. "If not," he adds, "we could expect to get worked over." The managers also learned by seeing what their peers were doing.

The tradition continues today for any number of good reasons. These inspection tours assure that all stores in the systems meet the company's high standards, that executives and board members enhance their understanding of the local stores, and finally that the store managers—no matter how geographically distant—feel like an integral part of the Westlake family.

The Golden Saw

Ribbon-cutting is for businesses without imagination. In the
Westlake tradition, the scissors have yielded to a golden saw, and the
ribbon has been replaced by a ceremonial board. Westlake officers
make a point to visit Grand Openings and christen each store
in style.

When the saw was first used, each store's opening
date was engraved in the blade. However it soon became
apparent that the blade would not be big enough
to document the ever-growing Westlake
network, and that practice ceased.

The gold isn't exactly real, of course,
but the ceremony is genuine, as are
the business practices that guide
each and every new store.

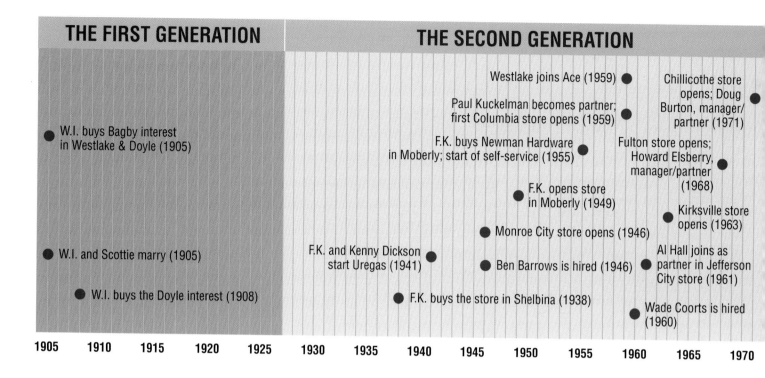

THE FIRST GENERATION

- W.I. buys Bagby interest in Westlake & Doyle (1905)
- W.I. and Scottie marry (1905)
- W.I. buys the Doyle interest (1908)

THE SECOND GENERATION

- Westlake joins Ace (1959)
- Chillicothe store opens; Doug Burton, manager/partner (1971)
- Paul Kuckelman becomes partner; first Columbia store opens (1959)
- F.K. buys Newman Hardware in Moberly; start of self-service (1955)
- Fulton store opens; Howard Elsberry, manager/partner (1968)
- F.K. opens store in Moberly (1949)
- Monroe City store opens (1946)
- Kirksville store opens (1963)
- F.K. and Kenny Dickson start Uregas (1941)
- Ben Barrows is hired (1946)
- Al Hall joins as partner in Jefferson City store (1961)
- F.K. buys the store in Shelbina (1938)
- Wade Coorts is hired (1960)

1905 1910 1915 1920 1925 1930 1935 1940 1945 1950 1955 1960 1965 1970

Westlake preserves this legacy not for its own sake but because it helps the company profit. Management, in fact, prides itself on returning a substantial and consistent profit on the investment that the shareholders have made in the company. The strategy that the company follows to ensure profitability works well in the brave new big-box era and resonates with the company's century-old tradition.

That strategy involves playing to the company's strengths: choosing sites wisely and continually perfecting that ability to do so; clustering stores in a relatively tight geographical area to exploit the strength of the Westlake name and to profit from economies of scale; and recruiting and training the kind of staff who will honor the Westlake tradition of sincere and competent service.

At century's end, Westlake Hardware boasts of 80 stores in six different regions: Mid-Missouri, Kansas City, Western Kansas, Omaha, Oklahoma, and Texas. There are currently 1,700 Westlake associates serving customers. This is a

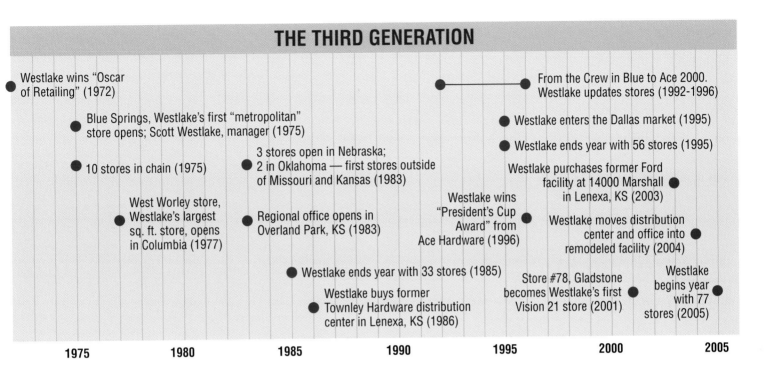

THE THIRD GENERATION

Westlake wins "Oscar of Retailing" (1972)

Blue Springs, Westlake's first "metropolitan" store opens; Scott Westlake, manager (1975)

10 stores in chain (1975)

3 stores open in Nebraska; 2 in Oklahoma — first stores outside of Missouri and Kansas (1983)

West Worley store, Westlake's largest sq. ft. store, opens in Columbia (1977)

Regional office opens in Overland Park, KS (1983)

Westlake ends year with 33 stores (1985)

Westlake buys former Townley Hardware distribution center in Lenexa, KS (1986)

From the Crew in Blue to Ace 2000. Westlake updates stores (1992-1996)

Westlake enters the Dallas market (1995)

Westlake ends year with 56 stores (1995)

Westlake purchases former Ford facility at 14000 Marshall in Lenexa, KS (2003)

Westlake wins "President's Cup Award" from Ace Hardware (1996)

Westlake moves distribution center and office into remodeled facility (2004)

Store #78, Gladstone becomes Westlake's first Vision 21 store (2001)

Westlake begins year with 77 stores (2005)

1975   1980   1985   1990   1995   2000   2005

part of the world where quality service is expected and rewarded and where tradition still matters. Westlake Hardware fits here well.

That tradition marches on. In 2005, a century into its history, Westlake Hardware is not slowing down but speeding up, adding at least four new stores in its centennial year—a pace that it intends to maintain.

One can never say for sure what tomorrow will bring, but if the first century foretells the second, one can be certain that Westlake's future will be a fair and proud and honorable one.

100 years old and still growing

Westlake's Hardware continues to grow by leaps and bounds. In fact, on the same day—April 21, 2005—two stores held Grand Openings, a first in Westlake history. At left, Howard Elsberry cuts the ceremonial board for Store #85 in Oklahoma City, Oklahoma (store shown above).

Below, Doug Burton wields the gold saw at the Store #86 in Mustang, Oklahoma.

Something for everyone

As these photographs from both Oklahoma events show, Westlake Grand Openings are well attended by the public. With activities for children, grand prize drawings and well-advertised sales, attendance is "standing room only."

(Left) Store #86 in Mustang continues to draw in customers as the days' events wind down.

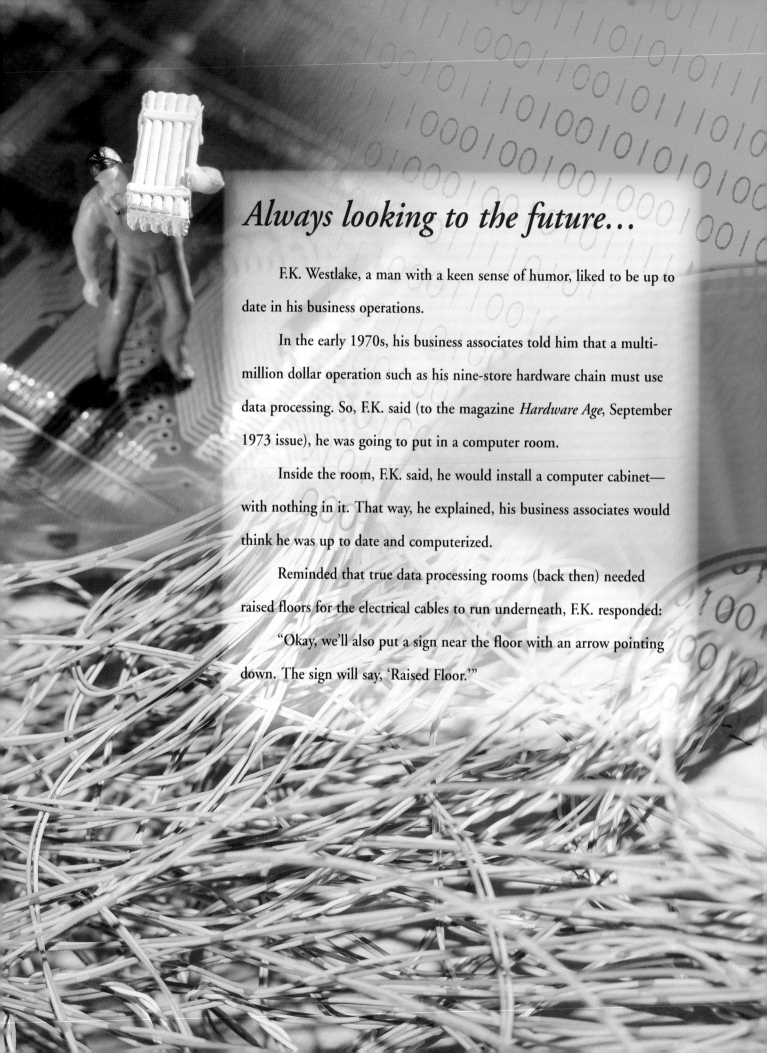

Always looking to the future...

F.K. Westlake, a man with a keen sense of humor, liked to be up to date in his business operations.

In the early 1970s, his business associates told him that a multi-million dollar operation such as his nine-store hardware chain must use data processing. So, F.K. said (to the magazine *Hardware Age*, September 1973 issue), he was going to put in a computer room.

Inside the room, F.K. said, he would install a computer cabinet—with nothing in it. That way, he explained, his business associates would think he was up to date and computerized.

Reminded that true data processing rooms (back then) needed raised floors for the electrical cables to run underneath, F.K. responded:

"Okay, we'll also put a sign near the floor with an arrow pointing down. The sign will say, 'Raised Floor.'"

Appendix

 **Hardware**
 **BRINKMANN** ®
 **BLACK&DECKER** ®
BOSCH

 **ARROW**
 **Alco**
 DAP ®
BUFFALO BRAND
Kwikset ®
A **BLACK&DECKER** COMPANY

 **CP** COLGATE-PALMOLIVE COMPANY

KRYLON ®

E&B Giftware

DURACELL ®

 **DeWALT**
High Performance Industrial Tools

HOT SHOT ®

Dix Greenhouse Inc.

In appreciation

*Westlake Hardware
recognizes these vendors
who have contributed to our
successful 100 years of
"helping America help itself."*

 **EVEREADY** ®

 **FORNEY**
INDUSTRIES, INC.

First Alert
...Because your family comes first!

 **SC Johnson**
A family company

GREEN COUNTRY SOIL

Quality Organic Soil Medias

 **HILLMAN**

 **Gilmour** ®
VERMONT AMERICAN CORPORATION

KAYTEE

IRWIN ®
Industrial Tools

 **ACE** Paint

Nicholson ®

 **KIDDE**
SAFETY

 Home Casual

Lufkin

 **K-R TOOLS**

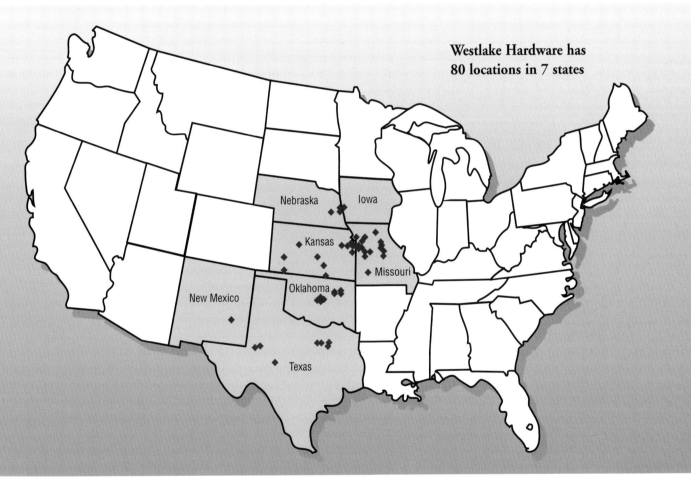

Westlake Hardware has 80 locations in 7 states

Nebraska · Iowa · Kansas · Missouri · New Mexico · Oklahoma · Texas

A Huntsville legacy

Westlake Hardware has been such an integral part of Huntsville, Missouri, that in March 2005 the Huntsville Historical Society sponsored a production that reenacted the history of the hardware company. Local fifth-graders were the star performers. Surely, W.I., Scottie, F.K., and other departed "Westlake family members" were present in spirit that night.

Local student David Kruse is shown at the Huntsville Historical Society which is housed in the former location of the first Westlake Hardware Store that opened in 1905.

Westlake's anniversary recognized by community

The Huntsville Historical Society hosted a play, "100 Years of Westlake Hardware." Area fifth-graders portrayed the various characters who played important parts in Westlake history. The play was performed on March 15, 2005, in the Westran Grade School gymnasium in Huntsville.